RABBLES, RIOTS, AND RUINS

MIKE AQUILINA

Rabbles, Riots, and Ruins

Twelve Ancient Cities and How They Were Evangelized

IGNATIUS PRESS   SAN FRANCISCO

Cover art and design by Enrique J. Aguilar

© 2024 by Ignatius Press, San Francisco
All rights reserved
ISBN 978-1-62164-678-5 (PB)
ISBN 978-1-64229-295-4 (eBook)
Library of Congress Control Number 2024931039
Printed in the United States of America ♾

For Vittorio

CONTENTS

ACKNOWLEDGMENTS

As always, I thank the pioneer webmasters Kevin Knight and Roger Pearse, who have for decades allowed me to use and adapt their e-texts for my books. Most of the sources I've cited come from nineteenth-century translations of the Church Fathers found on these men's websites: NewAdvent.org and Tertullian.org, respectively. The translations I use most often come from the Edinburgh edition of the *Ante-Nicene Fathers* (*ANF*) and *Nicene and Post-Nicene Fathers* (*NPNF*), which can be found among other resources at those sites. May God bless Messrs. Pearse and Knight abundantly for their generosity.

I am grateful to the good people at Ignatius Press—Paul Senz and Mark Brumley—for inviting me to write this book. I am indebted to Laura Shoemaker for making sure I finished it. The peerless editing team of Kathy Mosier and Darlene Broussard kept me from looking like a fool, and for that I thank them.

The producer of my podcast (*Way of the Fathers*), Thomas Mirus, gave me an opportunity to develop ideas in the open air and get immediate responses from listeners. Their comments helped make the finished product much better than it would have been. The book took its beginning from the podcast's third series, though the material here is much expanded and sometimes unrecognizable.

My dear and longtime friend Chris Bailey helped me find the most obscure sources—and provided translations from ancient and modern languages. I can never thank him enough.

And my wife, Terri, inspired me.

I praise God from whom all blessings flow.

Any errors herein are mine alone.

INTRODUCTION

They hardly dare to look at one another as they file into the church. They hardly even dare to look at the church. Most people have their eyes on the ground. They've already heard the bad news, and they assume it can only get worse.

What will happen to them? Any way they look at it, their lives are over. A few malcontents—well, all right, quite a few malcontents—went rampaging through the streets, and they pulled down the statues of the emperor and his family. Now the emperor is furious, and Theodosius is not an emperor you want to see when he's furious. He might order the whole city demolished. He might sell the citizens as slaves. He might massacre thousands of them indiscriminately.

But already the imperial commissioners have delivered the worst sentence a city could possibly suffer. Antioch will no longer be a *city*. It may still be a big cluster of buildings with a bunch of people in it, but as a *city* it will be dead. It won't have a municipal government. It won't be counted as one of the cities that make up the empire.

After that, a massacre would almost be a mercy.

Why Cities?

When prophets give us images of the life to come, they show us a heavenly city. The whole Bible ends with a glorious vision of the New Jerusalem: "Then I saw a new heaven and a new earth; for the first heaven and the first earth had passed away, and the sea was no more. And I saw the holy city, new Jerusalem, coming down out of heaven from God, prepared as a bride adorned for her husband; and I heard a great voice from the throne saying, 'Behold, the dwelling of God is with men'" (Rev 21:1–3).

It's a city with towering walls, laid out in a perfectly rational square, with gates that are never shut. The river of the water of life flows down the main street, and groves of the tree of life grow along the river, and there is no need for illumination because there is never any night. In other words, the New Jerusalem has none of the inconveniences we associate with cities. But it's definitely a city.

The whole Book of Revelation ends with a curse on anyone who takes anything away from the book: "God will take away his share in the tree of life and in the holy city, which are described in this book" (22:19). The worst thing that could possibly happen to you is that you'll be left out of the *city*, which is the place where the tree of life grows now.

Why is heaven a city? Why not a big, happy farm, or an unspoiled forest—or even a garden, like the garden where human life began in Genesis?

The answer goes deep into our traditions, Western and Eastern.

Start with what it means to be *civilized*. The word "civilization" means "creating cities".

Rightly or wrongly, we always give the city credit for everything we think of as "civilized": art, culture, literature, and of course politics—which also means life in cities, from the Greek word for a city, "polis".

For Christians, the idea of the city has a special resonance. Jerusalem was the seat of the worship of the true

God in the time before Christ; Jerusalem was where our redemption was accomplished. The image of heaven is formed on Jerusalem—a perfected Jerusalem, not the place with the smelly alleys and chronic water-supply problems but still recognizably a city.

Christianity began as a religion associated with cities. In fact, the word "pagan" originally meant a "country dweller". Later it came to mean someone who stuck to the old religion, because most of those people—so the urban Christians would have said, anyway—were ignorant bumpkins from the country.

Of course, history doesn't always fall into the tidy patterns that would make historians' jobs easy, but as a general rule Christianity came first to the cities. It makes sense: cities were built where they were because they were accessible. They were on major sea or land routes, and any traveler who came to a new province would end up in a city first. Any traveler who was bursting with good news would spill it first in a city.

The Book of Revelation, where we see heaven portrayed as a glorious city, begins with messages to the churches in seven cities—Patmos, Smyrna, Pergamum, Thyatira, Sardis, Philadelphia, and Laodicea. These were all substantial cities in Asia Minor, modern Turkey, and they certainly weren't the only ones. Two others might come to mind right away: Ephesus, where there was a church to which Saint Paul wrote a letter, and Tarsus, "no mean city" according to Saint Paul (Acts 21:39), who came from there and was proud of it.

In the New Testament, then, we see that Christians tended to see the world as a sprinkling of cities across the face of the land. But this was not just a Christian point of view. The Christians thought of the world that way because that was the way the Roman world thought of itself.

The Roman Empire was governed more or less as an association of cities. This is the key to understanding a lot of what we read about in history.

For example, a city that had a destructive riot might be punished—there might even be indiscriminate massacres of its residents. They were all guilty, because the city was guilty as a unit. When Paul was in Ephesus, for example, he provoked a near riot by the silversmiths who made souvenirs for the pilgrims to the shrine of Artemis there (see Acts 19:23–41). When the "town clerk" (19:35) calmed the crowd down, he told them, "For we are in danger of being charged with rioting today, there being no cause that we can give to justify this commotion" (19:40). This was apparently enough to make the mob go home. They had been reminded that the whole city could suffer if there was a breach of the peace.

On the other hand, even under the emperors we usually think of as the crazy ones—like Nero or Caligula—life might be very comfortable and secure across most of the empire. That was because the emperor wasn't doing the day-to-day governing. Most of the government that people actually came into contact with was the government in their local town or city—a government they themselves had some influence over. Rome was no longer a republic, but the empire was in its way a collection of thousands of little republics. By one ancient count, the Roman Empire was made up of 5,627 local municipalities.[1]

Each of these cities usually controlled a certain part of the countryside around it. This was where the rich had their factory farms and their summer estates; it was where fresh produce for the city dwellers came from. Generally,

---

[1] James S. Reid, *The Municipalities of the Roman Empire* (Cambridge: Cambridge University Press, 1913), p. 4.

when you passed out of the control of one city, you passed into the control of another.

Start at the Synagogue

Now we understand it a little better when the Acts of the Apostles gives us a picture of the Christian faith spreading from city to city. And in every city, the Apostles start at the synagogue. The rest of history seems to bear out this picture. We can't always put names to the first Christians who evangelized in a particular place. Except for the people mentioned in Acts, and a few bare names in Paul's letters, that first generation is mostly anonymous. But in every city in the Roman Empire, Christians seem to have begun with the synagogue.

This was because they saw themselves as fulfilling the Jewish tradition, not forming a new religion. They began with the people they thought of as their own, trying to show them that the law and the prophets had been fulfilled, just as Moses, Isaiah, and the rest had promised.

Every city of any size had a Jewish community. This was partly because Jews in Roman times were enterprising traders and travelers, but probably even more because every city had some people from everywhere in the Roman Empire.

Wherever there was a Jewish community, there was a synagogue, or more than one synagogue if the community was large.

The Temple was in Jerusalem, and that was the center of Jewish worship (until it was destroyed in the year 70). It was the only place where sacrifices could be offered to God. But it wasn't possible for a Jew in Rome or Alexandria or Carthage to get to Jerusalem very often. Thus, the Jewish communities built synagogues—meeting places where Jews would gather to hear the Scriptures read and explained, in a way very much like our Liturgy of the Word, where we hear the Scripture lessons and a homily about them.

One thing that seems to have been a regular feature of synagogue meetings was inviting interesting travelers to speak a few words of wisdom. When Jesus came home to Nazareth, for example, he was invited to read the Scripture and interpret it:

> And he stood up to read; and there was given to him the book of the prophet Isaiah. He opened the book and found the place where it was written, "The Spirit of the Lord is upon me, because he has anointed me to preach good news to the poor. He has sent me to proclaim release to the captives and recovering of sight to the blind, to set at liberty those who are oppressed, to proclaim the acceptable year of the Lord." And he closed the book, and gave it back to the attendant, and sat down; and the eyes of all in the synagogue were fixed on him. And he began to say to them, "Today this Scripture has been fulfilled in your hearing." (Lk 4:16–21)

When the Apostles were spreading the Good News, they made use of this tradition wherever they went. Paul, for example, was invited to speak in the synagogue at Pisidian Antioch: "And on the sabbath day they went into the synagogue and sat down. After the reading of the law and the prophets, the rulers of the synagogue sent to them, saying, 'Brethren, if you have any word of exhortation for the people, say it.' So Paul stood up, and motioning with his hand said: 'Men of Israel, and you that fear God, listen'" (Acts 13:14–16).

We see the same thing throughout Paul's journeys: "At Iconium they entered together into the Jewish synagogue"

(14:1). At Thessalonica, "Paul went in, as was his custom, and for three weeks he argued with them from the Scriptures" (17:2). At Beroea, "when [Paul and Silas] arrived they went into the Jewish synagogue" (17:10). At Athens, "he argued in the synagogue with the Jews and the devout persons" (17:17). At Corinth, "he argued in the synagogue every sabbath, and persuaded Jews and Greeks" (18:4). At Ephesus, "he entered the synagogue and for three months spoke boldly, arguing and pleading about the kingdom of God" (19:8).

When the Acts of the Apostles mentions these synagogues, we sometimes see two groups of people: "Jews" and "devout persons", or "Jews" and "Greeks". Here we see another important fact about the synagogues in cities across the Roman Empire: there were many people who were not Jews who nevertheless worshiped God and came to the synagogue to hear the Scriptures. These "God-fearers" were a big part of the first Christians' audience. From the Apostles they heard about the Way. They heard that the long-promised Messiah had come, and now there was no distinction between Jew and Greek. This was a very attractive proposition to people who had always been not quite full members of the synagogue. There were Gentile converts to Judaism in every city that had a synagogue, and it seems likely that many of them were among the earliest and most enthusiastic converts to the Way.

A Dozen Cities

So far we've seen what all the Roman cities had in common and how the early Christians made use of those commonalities to create an empire-wide strategy for spreading the Good News. But each city had its own individual culture

as well. Most of them predated the Roman Empire by centuries. They imported what they liked from the Romans,
but they kept their own ancient traditions as well.

Naturally, the Jewish communities in each of those cities developed in different ways—ways that reflected the
cultures of the cities around them. The Christian communities, in turn, came out of the Jewish communities
with some of their traditions, and Christians adapted to the
atmosphere of the city around them.

This is what makes it worth taking a closer look at some
of these cities. How did the Church come to be what it
is today? How did the differences between East and West
begin? Where did our most ancient traditions come from?
How did Catholic theology find its intellectual founda-
tions? If we want the answers to these questions, we have
to look at the different cities where the early Church grew
up. We have to understand what was different about them
as well as what they had in common.

We'll have more information when we're done, and
that information will be useful in understanding our faith.
But it's also going to be a lot of fun. There are mysteries to
solve, great stories to tell, and plenty of fascinating questions to think about.

So here's a dozen: a small selection of cities that were
important in early Christianity.

Jerusalem was the holy city to all faithful Jews, and it was
something almost unique in the Roman Empire: a city that
was important not simply because of its trade or its strategic location but because of its religious associations. The
Temple in Jerusalem was the only place where Jews could
offer sacrifices. For Christians, Jerusalem was the place
where Jesus had taught and died and risen from the dead. It
was also the first of these cities to be wiped completely off
the map.

Antioch was where the followers of the Way were first called "Christians" (Acts 11:26). It was the city of bright lights and broad streets, the most important place in the eastern provinces, one of the greatest cities in the empire. It was also a place that developed its own distinctive Christian culture, with its own distinctive way of interpreting Scripture. And from Antioch, we'll learn just how frightening it could be when the mob offended an emperor prone to temper tantrums.

Rome was the capital of the world, and it became the capital of the Church when Peter took up residence there. Pagan Rome was notorious for "shows" where dying Christians were the entertainment. Christian Rome faced barbarian invasions and emperors so weak that the popes finally had to do the emperor's job.

Alexandria in Egypt was the trading center of the East and the intellectual heart of the Mediterranean world, famous for the lighthouse—the Pharos, one of the Seven Wonders of the World—that guarded its gleaming harbor. The city had already developed a distinguished Jewish intellectual tradition when Christianity came along, and we'll see how the one tradition flowed right into the other. But in spite of its intellectual reputation, Alexandria was also notorious as a city of riots.

Ephesus was famous for another of the Seven Wonders— the Temple of Artemis (or Diana to the Romans). It was a big draw for tourists. In Acts 19, we find the only riot recorded in Scripture that was provoked by souvenir salesmen (see 19:21–41). But in Christian history, Ephesus is best known as the place where Jesus' mother spent her last years on earth.

Edessa, a city where Greek and Semitic cultures met, preserved a unique tradition. According to Edessan tradition, the king of Edessa corresponded with Jesus himself. Copies of the correspondence were kept in the city archives. Did King Abgar really get a letter from Jesus Christ?

Lugdunum, today's Lyon, in France, was the big city in Roman Gaul. It was a place where people and ideas from the East came into the West, and it developed its own Christian culture very early. As a defender of Catholic orthodoxy, one of its bishops left us an encyclopedia of non-Catholic Christian sects.

Ejmiatsin, or Etchmiadzin, or Vagharshapat, is the spiritual center of Armenia—a place few of us in the West spend much time thinking about. But Armenia has an honored position in Christian history as the first officially Christian country, and the Ejmiatsin Cathedral is the oldest standing cathedral in the world. We'll find out that, from our particular point of view, Armenia is even more important as the country that preserved many ancient works of Christian literature when they were lost to the rest of the world.

Constantinople was founded by the first Christian emperor as the new capital of the empire. It quickly became a giant metropolis—and, as the imperial capital of the East, the place where the constant battle between church and state provided endless drama. Bishops and emperors and empresses and scheming government officials played out a constant soap opera, with the grumbling mob in the background always threatening to burn down the city.

Milan is the fashion capital of Italy today. In the 300s, it was the western capital of the empire, growing to overshadow even Rome in importance. In Christian history, it's probably most famous as the city whose bishop shamed one of Rome's most powerful emperors into public penance.

Ravenna became the capital of the Western Roman Empire in the period of barbarian invasions. Protected by sea on one side and marsh on the other, it was a good place for a weak emperor to cower while the barbarians had their way with Rome and other important cities. After the last Western emperor retired, it became the Byzantine Empire's foothold in Italy, so that today some of the most important Eastern Christian art is in the West.

Carthage, the big city of North Africa, was one of the most important centers of Latin culture. Many of the greatest writers of classical times, both pagan and Christian, came from Carthage or the area around it. For Western Christians, Carthage holds a special place: at a time when Roman Christians still used Greek in the liturgy, our Latin Rite began not in Rome but in Africa.

These are the fascinating places we will visit in the pages that follow. Each one has its unique points of interest. We'll climb their hills, sail into their harbors, walk down their streets, push our way through their bustling markets. We'll look up in awe at their titanic public works and smell the stench of their sewers (fortunately only metaphorically). And we'll see how all those things shaped the expression, practice, and history of the Christianity we know today. Along the way, we'll meet some of the most famous Fathers of the Church. We'll hear a few funny stories. Maybe, once in a while, we will run into an angel.

And, by the way, we'll hear how that story of Antioch has an almost miraculously happy ending.

These certainly aren't the only important places in early Christian history. It was hard whittling down the list to just this many. What about Corinth, with its constantly feuding church that caused Paul no end of headaches? What about Eboracum, all the way up in the northern end of Britain, which gave the Roman world its first Christian emperor? What about Thessalonica? What about Bethlehem?

But we have to stop somewhere or the book will never end. And since we have to start somewhere too, let's start with Jerusalem, the holy city. What made Jerusalem so special?

I

Jerusalem

The words of an anonymous poet from the time of the
Exile tell us more about Jerusalem than we could learn
from hundreds of pages of academic study. They tell us
how the people of Jerusalem felt about their city:

> If I forget you, O Jerusalem,
>   let my right hand wither!
> Let my tongue cleave to the roof of my mouth,
>   if I do not remember you,
> if I do not set Jerusalem
>   above my highest joy! (Ps 137:5–6)

All over the world, people are proud of the cities they
live in. We'll see that over and over in this book: ancient
writers pointing out the mighty works of engineering,
the fabulous temples, the ships in the harbor, the travelers
assembling from all nations. These are the things that make
a great city great, and they've always been sources of pride
for the people who live in those cities.

But no city was ever loved the way Jerusalem was loved.

Let's put the words of the psalmist in context. In the year
587 B.C., the Babylonians destroyed Jerusalem, the capital
of the troublesome little kingdom of Judah. All the survivors were deported to far-off Babylon—a much bigger and
much more magnificent city. But it wasn't Jerusalem.

The exiled people of Judah must have made an instantly identifiable minority in the big city. That same psalm begins with these famous words:

> By the waters of Babylon,
>   there we sat down and wept,
>   when we remembered Zion.
> On the willows there
>   we hung up our lyres.
> For there our captors
>   required of us songs,
> and our tormentors, mirth, saying,
>   "Sing us one of the songs of Zion!" (Ps 137:1–3)

The "songs of Zion" must have been a popular form of entertainment for the privileged Babylonians—the ones who could afford to have a servant from Judah working for them. And we can see why the songs of Zion were so famous. We still sing them today. This is one of them.

Before David

Jerusalem, the City of David, is so much identified with the people of Israel that we forget it wasn't originally an Israelite city at all. Like many cities in Israel, it was a Canaanite city at first. But unlike most of the other cities, it held out against the advancing Israelites.

The first time we hear about a city named Salem is in the story of Abram (later Abraham) when Melchizedek, king of Salem, blesses Abram (see Gen 14:17–24). Abram's nephew Lot was living in Sodom, and after a battle of petty kings, Sodom was sacked and Lot was taken along with all the movable possessions (see 14:1–12). Abram went to the rescue of his nephew, routed the victors, and brought back all the captives and loot (see 14:13–16). "Melchizedek king of Salem brought out bread and wine; he was priest of God Most High. And he blessed him and said, 'Blessed be Abram by God Most High, maker of heaven and earth; and blessed be God Most High, who has delivered your enemies into your hand!' And Abram gave him a tenth of everything" (14:18–20).

There's already something special about this Salem, later to be known as Jerusalem. The king there is also a priest, and he is a "priest of God Most High", clearly identified in this story as the same God who had called Abram out of Ur of the Chaldees to the Promised Land. And he brings out bread and wine.[1]

His name would come up again in a psalm attributed to David:

> The LORD has sworn
>   and will not change his mind,
> "You are a priest for ever
>   according to the order of Melchizedek." (110:4)

The Israelites would later have a priesthood that belonged to one tribe—the Levites. But David was from the tribe of Judah. He couldn't be a priest of the Levitical order, but Melchizedek was a priest of God Most High before Levi, founder of the tribe of the Levites, was even born.

Christians would see this as an obvious precursor of the priesthood of Christ, who was a descendant of David and

[1] That's the traditional identification, anyway, and accepted by most modern scholars. Some scholars point to a different town as Melchizedek's Salem, but what's most important is that Jews and Christians have believed for many centuries that it was the same place as Jerusalem.

thus also from the tribe of Judah. "For this Melchizedek, king of Salem, priest of the Most High God, met Abraham returning from the slaughter of the kings and blessed him; and to him Abraham apportioned a tenth part of everything. He is first, by translation of his name, king of righteousness, and then he is also king of Salem, that is, king of peace. He is without father or mother or genealogy, and has neither beginning of days nor end of life, but resembling the Son of God he continues a priest for ever" (Heb 7:1–3).

This gave Christ's priesthood roots that went back before the Law of Moses—back to the mysterious king of Salem.

Kicking Out the Jebusites

When Joshua led the Israelites into the Promised Land, they were very successful against most of their Canaanite enemies. But a few held out. "The people of Benjamin did not drive out the Jebusites who dwelt in Jerusalem; so the Jebusites have dwelt with the people of Benjamin in Jerusalem to this day", says the Book of Judges (1:21), indicating that it was written before King David conquered the city.

In the story of the Levite's concubine in Judges 19, we read that the Levite and his servant "arrived opposite Jebus (that is, Jerusalem)" (19:10). And "when they were near Jebus, the day was far spent, and the servant said to his master, 'Come now, let us turn aside to this city of the Jebusites, and spend the night in it.' And his master said to him, 'We will not turn aside into the city of foreigners, who do not belong to the sons of Israel; but we will pass on to Gibe-ah" (19:11–12).

So Jerusalem was a foreign land in the middle of Israel. It remained foreign through the reign of Saul, the first king of Israel.

But then came David.

When David became king, his capital was Hebron. But something started a fight with the Jebusites, and they taunted David with the inaccessibility of their city.

> And the king and his men went to Jerusalem against the Jebusites, the inhabitants of the land, who said to David, "You will not come in here, but the blind and the lame will ward you off"—thinking, "David cannot come in here." Nevertheless David took the stronghold of Zion, that is, the city of David. And David said on that day, "Whoever would strike the Jebusites, let him get up the water shaft to attack the lame and the blind, who are hated by David's soul." Therefore it is said, "The blind and the lame shall not come into the house." And David dwelt in the stronghold, and called it the city of David. (2 Sam 5:6–9)

When the Jebusites tell David that "the blind and the lame will ward you off", they're probably saying that their city is so impregnable that it could be defended by the blind and the lame—although the saying is obscure enough that various traditions rose to explain it in other convoluted ways. David responds by picking up the insult and turning it back on the Jebusites.

The old part of Jerusalem—the part that became known as the City of David—does in fact sit on a site that is hard to reach. Precipitous slopes make it one of the most defensible of ancient cities.

But they also give the city a big problem to solve: water. There wasn't a good natural source of water inside the city, and some arrangement had to be made for bringing in water from outside, even when the city was under siege.

David's men took advantage of the Jebusites' water shaft to sneak into the city. (Modern archaeologists have found a Bronze Age channel, already ancient in David's time, that men could walk through.) So, about a thousand years before Christ, David finally captured the Canaanite hold-out city of Jerusalem.

Once David had taken Jerusalem, he made it his capital and immediately set about improving it. "David built the city round about from the Millo inward.... And Hiram king of Tyre sent messengers to David, and cedar trees, also carpenters and masons who built David a house" (2 Sam 5:9, 11). Finally, David brought the Ark of the Covenant to Jerusalem, making it the religious center of Israel. It became "the place which the LORD your God will choose, to make his name dwell there" (Deut 12:11), as Moses had been told: "You shall seek the place which the LORD your God will choose out of all your tribes to put his name and make his habitation there; there you shall go, and there you shall bring your burnt offerings and your sacrifices.... Take heed that you do not offer your burnt offerings at every place that you see; but at the place which the LORD will choose in one of your tribes, there you shall offer your burnt offerings, and there you shall do all that I am commanding you" (12:5–6, 13–14).

From then on, sacrifices to God could be offered only at Jerusalem.

Surrounded by Enemies

King David built himself a fine palace with cedars of Lebanon imported from Tyre, but it was left to his son Solomon to build the Temple, a permanent place of worship for the God of Israel. To later writers, this was one of the central events of history. The two books of Chronicles devote twelve chapters to David's preparations for the Temple, Solomon's building of it, and the dedication ceremonies. Nothing else since the giving of the Law to Moses had received such a full treatment in the historical books.

So at last there was a Temple in Jerusalem, the place where God's Name dwelt, and all the people of Israel came and offered their sacrifices there. And this happy situation lasted for exactly one reign. When Solomon died, his clumsy son Rehoboam provoked a rebellion in which most of Israel went its own way, leaving Rehoboam with Jerusalem and the stubby little Kingdom of Judah (see 1 Kings 12:1–15). But how would the people of Israel, the larger Northern Kingdom, get into enemy territory to make their sacrifices? Jeroboam, the rebel king, wasn't going to let that happen.

> Jeroboam said in his heart, "Now the kingdom will turn back to the house of David; if this people go up to offer sacrifices in the house of the LORD at Jerusalem, then the heart of this people will turn again to their lord, to Rehoboam king of Judah, and they will kill me and return to Rehoboam king of Judah." So the king took counsel, and made two calves of gold. And he said to the people, "You have gone up to Jerusalem long enough. Behold your gods, O Israel, who brought you up out of the land of Egypt." (12:26–28)

Thus, idolatry came roaring back for most of Israel, and most of the history of the Northern Kingdom, as written by the partisans of the God of Israel, is a history of the small minority of God's prophets warning the majority, who worshiped Baal and other popular deities, that they were headed for a bad time.

Their predictions came true. The Northern Kingdom was wiped out by Assyria, an empire with a Stalinist policy of moving whole populations away from their homeland to stamp out local patriotism. All the important people were taken away from Israel and resettled God knows where, and that was the end of the Northern Kingdom— the "ten lost tribes".

What was left was Judah, which escaped Assyrian conquest by the skin of its teeth. Judah also fell into idolatry most of the time, but every once in a while, a reforming king would come to the throne and take the prophets' warnings seriously. Hezekiah was one of them.

Jerusalem grew enormously during the time of Hezekiah—but the growth was not a sign of prosperity. The city ballooned as it absorbed refugees from the ever-encroaching Assyrians. Hezekiah responded by improving the water supply with a new tunnel and reservoir. He "made the pool and the conduit and brought water into the city" (2 Kings 20:20), addressing the same problem the ancient Jebusites had already faced with their water shaft, but on a larger scale.[2]

By Hezekiah's time, the Assyrian Empire had itself been conquered, and the Babylonian Empire was the power to worry about. Judah was an absurdly small power to stand up against mighty Babylon, and Babylon knew it. In the reign of Jehoiachin, the Babylonian king Nebuchadnezzar conquered Jerusalem, took the king and the leading citizens off to Babylon, and made Jehoiachin's uncle Zedekiah his puppet king in Jerusalem.

But even then Jerusalem kept rebelling.

---

[2] Magen Broshi, "The Inhabitants of Jerusalem", in *City of the Great King: Jerusalem from David to the Present*, ed. Nitza Rosovsky (Cambridge, Mass.: Harvard University Press, 1996), p. 14.

Finally, the Babylonians had had enough. On the Ninth of Ab in the year 587 B.C., Nebuchadnezzar's army burned the city, including the Temple, the palaces, and "every great house" (25:9).

After Babylon

Babylon itself was not a permanent fixture, however. Just as Babylon had conquered Assyria, a new rising empire conquered Babylon. In 539 B.C., the Persians marched in, and a new emperor was in charge.

This emperor, Cyrus, was different from the other conquerors, and his empire was different from the other empires. Instead of trying to integrate the whole empire as one unit by shuffling around populations to break up local patriotism, the Persians allowed their conquered provinces to keep most of their local customs and even their local governments. It was a kind of federal empire: as long as the tax money kept flowing to the central government, the provinces had a lot of freedom.

The year after he conquered Babylon, Cyrus decreed that any Judean who wanted to go back could return to Jerusalem. He even put up government money for restoring the city and the Temple. This was typical Persian government policy, but it was a miracle to the exiled Jews. It was the work of God, "who says of Cyrus, 'He is my shepherd, and he shall fulfil all my purpose'; saying of Jerusalem, 'She shall be built,' and of the temple, 'Your foundation shall be laid'" (Is 44:28).

These straggling returnees moved back into Jerusalem, but they didn't prosper. We know that from the Book of Nehemiah: "Now it happened in the month of Chislev, in the twentieth year, as I was in Susa the capital, that Hanani, one of my brethren, came with certain men out of Judah; and I asked them concerning the Jews that survived, who had escaped exile, and concerning Jerusalem" (1:1–2).

The news he got was not good: "And they said to me, 'The survivors there in the province who escaped exile are in great trouble and shame; the wall of Jerusalem is broken down, and its gates are destroyed by fire.' When I heard these words I sat down and wept, and mourned for days; and I continued fasting and praying before the God of heaven" (1:3–4).

Fortunately for Jerusalem, Nehemiah was in a high position in the court of the Persian emperor, and he wasn't afraid to speak his mind. He persuaded the emperor to let him go to Jerusalem and rebuild it.

But he had heard enough of the reports from Jerusalem to know that he would have to be careful. It was surrounded by people who had been living in Judah while the Jews were in exile and who weren't too happy about these people coming back from Babylon. Nehemiah took a secret tour by night and left us an eyewitness account of what the city had looked like when the exiles started returning:

> I came to Jerusalem and was there three days. Then I arose in the night, I and a few men with me; and I told no one what my God had put into my heart to do for Jerusalem. There was no beast with me but the beast on which I rode. I went out by night by the Valley Gate to the Jackal's Well and to the Dung Gate, and I inspected the walls of Jerusalem which were broken down and its gates which had been destroyed by fire. Then I went on to the Fountain Gate and to the King's Pool; but there was no place for the beast that was under me to pass. Then I went up in the night by the valley and inspected the wall; and I turned back and entered by the Valley Gate, and so returned. (2:11–15)

Jerusalem was a tiny city in Nehemiah's time; most of the expansions of Hezekiah's reign were abandoned, and the city was back to the size it had been in the time of the Jebusites.[3] Even in that tiny town, there was a lot of open space, because only a few people lived there (see 7:4).

Nevertheless, the city was rebuilt on a smaller scale, and the foundation of a new Temple was laid. It was a joyous occasion, with trumpets and cheers. But there were people there who remembered the Temple of Solomon, and this one was much smaller.

> All the people shouted with a great shout, when they praised the LORD, because the foundation of the house of the LORD was laid. But many of the priests and Levites and heads of fathers' houses, old men who had seen the first house, wept with a loud voice when they saw the foundation of this house being laid, though many shouted aloud for joy; so that the people could not distinguish the sound of the joyful shout from the sound of the people's weeping, for the people shouted with a great shout, and the sound was heard afar. (Ezra 3:11–13)

Herod the Great

After the revolt of the Maccabees, a new Jewish kingdom was established in 164 B.C. Now Jerusalem expanded again, beginning to look once more like a real capital city.

And then came Herod—King Herod the Great, to give him the slightly sarcastic name history has left him with. This was the same Herod who tried to kill the infant Messiah by murdering all male children two years old and younger in Bethlehem. He was a client of the Romans, who decreed him king and allowed him a certain measure

[3] Ibid.

of independence that was fuzzily defined. He was para-
noid and cruel—he had three of his own sons executed.
But he was scrupulous about keeping to the Jewish dietary
laws: no pork ever touched his lips. The emperor Augustus famously remarked that he would rather be Herod's
pig than Herod's son.

Herod loved big buildings and magnificent construc-
tions of all sorts. The Jewish historian Josephus tells us
how Herod tore into Jerusalem with a zeal for architecture
unlike anything the city had seen since Solomon's time.

Accordingly, in the fifteenth year of his reign, Herod
rebuilt the Temple and closed in a piece of land around
it with a wall, which was twice as large as that before
enclosed. The expenses he incurred for it were enormous,
and the magnificence was never surpassed, as evidenced by
the great colonnades that were erected about the Temple
and the citadel that was on its north side. Herod built new
colonnades, but he repaired the citadel at vast expense.
It was nothing less than a royal palace, which he called
Antonia, in honor of Mark Antony, his powerful Roman
patron. He also built himself a palace in the upper city,
containing two very large and most beautiful sections, to
which the holy house itself could not be compared.[4]

Herod replaced the smaller Second Temple with a huge
new Temple that was one of the wonders of the age. Jerusalem became a capital city to rival the other provincial
capitals, with luxurious houses, paved streets, and even
good sewers.

Much of the improvement was financed by a half shekel
regularly collected from every adult male Jew everywhere

---

[4] Josephus, *Jewish War* 1.401–2, trans. H. St. J. Thackeray, M.A., in *Josephus*,
vol. 2, *The Jewish War, Books I–III* (Cambridge: Harvard University Press; London: William Heinemann, 1926), p. 189.

for the maintenance of the Temple, which was interpreted as including the city around it. Money was flowing into Jerusalem from all over the Roman Empire and beyond. Herod could afford to be extravagant. Nevertheless, he was more extravagant than he could afford to be, and when he wasn't building something or murdering his relatives, he was usually figuring out a new way to squeeze money out of his subjects.

Herod made Jerusalem into the great city that was the setting for the climax of the drama of salvation. What was it like to come into the city when Jesus was alive?

City of Pilgrims

Three times a year, pilgrims came to Jerusalem from all points and multiplied the population several times over: the feasts of Passover, Pentecost, and Booths, or Tabernacles. The roads were crowded with large groups traveling to Jerusalem for the festival and then leaving for home when it was over. Luke gives us a vivid picture of one pilgrim family's panic over losing their son on one of these trips: "His parents went to Jerusalem every year at the feast of the Passover. And when he was twelve years old, they went up according to custom; and when the feast was ended, as they were returning, the boy Jesus stayed behind in Jerusalem. His parents did not know it, but supposing him to be in the company they went a day's journey, and they sought him among their kinsfolk and acquaintances; and when they did not find him, they returned to Jerusalem, seeking him" (Lk 2:41-45). They found him in the Temple, of course, because the boy was Jesus.

How could Mary and Joseph be so careless? The answer was that they were "supposing him to be in the

company"—a great crowd of people they knew from
home who had all been up to Jerusalem and were on their
way back. They didn't worry at all.

So we can imagine ourselves part of a big crowd coming toward Jerusalem for one of the festivals. If we like,
we can even imagine ourselves coming in with the crowd
that travels with Jesus as he enters the city for the last time.

Before we even see the city, we can smell it.

Many cities have been known for their industrial smells,
but this one is different. Jerusalem smells delicious. Its biggest industry is animal sacrifice, so the smell of barbecue is
always in the air.

And then there it is, up on top of a hill, looking almost
halfway to heaven. The Temple with its gleaming stones
dominates the view, but the magnificent walls and palaces
are almost as impressive.

As we squash in with the crowd through one of the
gates, we feel as though we've left the mundane behind us.

Jerusalem was an ancient city with ancient memories,
but for small-town hicks like Jesus' disciples, one of the
most impressive things about it must have been how new
and up-to-date it was. It must have seemed like New York
in the 1930s or Dubai today—a place of modern architec-
tural wonders and heroic feats of engineering, where you
could see something amazing from every corner.

The big-city bustle is marvelous to us country folk too.
Everywhere people are going places and doing things. And
when we get to the Temple—which we do, of course,
because the reason anyone comes to Jerusalem is to visit
the Temple—we find the courtyards mobbed with buyers
and sellers.

When we get closer, we notice the price tags. Then we
discover another amazing thing about Jerusalem: it's shock-
ingly expensive. A pigeon is supposed to be the sacrifice

that the poor can afford to offer: "If he cannot afford a lamb, then he shall bring, as his guilt offering to the LORD for the sin which he has committed, two turtledoves or two young pigeons" (Lev 5:7). But here in Jerusalem, a pigeon may cost a hundred times what it costs in the country.[5] If you want your pigeon certified blemish free and sacrifice ready, it's going to cost you.

Now we understand it a little better when we see Jesus really angry one of the few times on record: "He entered the temple and began to drive out those who sold and those who bought in the temple, and he overturned the tables of the money-changers and the seats of those who sold pigeons; and he would not allow any one to carry anything through the temple. And he taught, and said to them, 'Is it not written, "My house shall be called a house of prayer for all the nations"? But you have made it a den of robbers'" (Mk 11:15–17).

As we listen to the haggling going on, we small-town hicks notice yet another astounding thing about this city: it's full of all kinds of people we've never seen before. "There were dwelling in Jerusalem Jews, devout men from every nation under heaven" (Acts 2:5).

The overwhelming majority of the people around us in Jerusalem are Jews. But Jews are a surprisingly diverse group of people. They've come from "every nation under heaven", and they speak all the languages of the different nations they come from. They are "Parthians and Medes and Elamites and residents of Mesopotamia, Judea and Cappadocia, Pontus and Asia, Phrygia and Pamphylia, Egypt and the parts of Libya belonging to Cyrene, and

---

[5] Joachim Jeremias, *Jerusalem in the Time of Jesus: An Investigation into Economic and Social Conditions during the New Testament Period* (Philadelphia: Fortress Press, 1969), p. 121.

visitors from Rome, both Jews and proselytes, Cretans and Arabians" (2:9–11).

What makes them all Jews is that they all believe Jerusalem is the place God has chosen as the center of his worship. Only in Jerusalem can the sacrifices to God be offered. Jews from the other end of the Roman Empire, or from outside the Roman Empire, have to come to Jerusalem to offer their sacrifices. Not all of them can go; there are doubtless Jews who live their whole lives in Spain or Britain who have never once seen Jerusalem. But any Jew who can possibly make it would want to visit Jerusalem at least once for Passover. All the visitors probably have the same reaction Jesus' disciples had: "Look, Teacher, what wonderful stones and what wonderful buildings!" (Mk 13:1).

But Jesus' reaction must have surprised everyone who heard it: "Do you see these great buildings? There will not be left here one stone upon another, that will not be thrown down" (13:2).

Or perhaps it didn't surprise them. They knew that Judea, the Roman province, was full of fanatics who wanted to end Roman rule at any cost. Perhaps Jesus just struck them as a pessimistic but clear-eyed observer of the political situation. Someday soon, there's going to be another war.

The Jewish War

In the year A.D. 64, Gessius Florus was appointed governor of Judea. He hated Jews and he hated Judea, but he was a friend of Nero's, and that got him the job. He immediately set about what looks like a deliberate experiment in seeing how much he could make his subjects hate him—taking huge bribes for hearing complaints and then jailing the complainants, stealing funds from the Temple, crucifying city leaders who were Roman citizens (and thus ineligible for crucifixion). If making all Judea hate him was the plan, it worked. Open rebellion broke out.

Nero, showing good sense for once in his life, sent his best general, Vespasian, to put down the rebellion. He quickly pacified the rest of Judea. Jerusalem held out.

During this time, according to Christian historians, the small Christian community was warned by a prophecy to leave Jerusalem. They went to a little town called Pella and waited for the fulfillment of Jesus' prophecy that not one stone would remain upon another.

They didn't have long to wait.

The rebels were surprisingly successful at first. But they had no good leaders and no strategy. They tried to harness the power of desperation by doing everything possible to damage their own position: they destroyed the food stocks in Jerusalem so that a long siege would be impossible. They destroyed large parts of the city.

Meanwhile, Vespasian was called off to be emperor. It was the Year of the Four Emperors (A.D. 69): Nero had been killed shortly after the Jewish War broke out, and one after another useless emperors succeeded him until the soldiers chose Vespasian, who stuck. He left his capable son Titus in charge of the siege of Jerusalem.

In spite of the fanatical defense, Titus did his best to be lenient toward the innocent civilians. More than once he offered to stop the battle in the city and go outside to fight. He even offered to stop the battle long enough to let the Jewish priests make their sacrifices. But the rebel leaders were determined to fight to the end. Possibly their early successes had convinced them they could win. Possibly they wanted to die now rather than later. At any rate,

Titus was humane and even kind by Roman standards, but he wasn't going to be a loser.

Even as the fighting raged, Titus tried to preserve the Temple, going against the advice he got from his commanders, who said the Judeans would always be rebellious as long as the Temple was standing. But Titus said it was an ornament to the whole empire. We can stop and think for a moment what a remarkable building Herod's Temple must have been if the Roman commander did his best to save it even when his enemies were using it as a fortress.

On the Ninth of Ab, the very day Nebuchadnezzar had burned Solomon's Temple, the last battle was fought and the Temple was burned. When Titus heard it was ablaze, he ran to the fire and tried to put it out. He ordered his soldiers to extinguish the flames, but they were winning now, and they were beyond control. The Temple was destroyed, and what was left of Jerusalem was destroyed with it.

Death and Rebirth of Jerusalem

The end of the Temple in A.D. 70 was the end of the Israelite sacrificial cult. The Jewish religion had to reimagine itself. Jerusalem was gone: it was just a Roman military camp now. Judaism had to focus on the local synagogues.

Christians saw the destruction of the Temple as the fulfillment of Jesus' prophecies. Not one stone was left upon another. Well, almost. One wall—the Western Wall—is still standing today. For traditional Jews, it is the holiest place in the world. It's often called the Wailing Wall, because that is where faithful Jews mourn the loss of the Temple and the holy city of Jerusalem.

In 130, the Roman emperor Hadrian decided to rebuild Jerusalem as a new pagan Roman city, Aelia Capitolina.

(Hadrian came from the Aelius family, and he dedicated his new city to the three pagan gods of the Capitolium in Rome: Jupiter, Juno, and Minerva.) This caused another bloody revolt; even in ruins, Jerusalem meant more to Jews than Hadrian could imagine. The revolt failed again, and Hadrian went ahead with his plans, trying to obliterate the memory of Jerusalem as a focus of Jewish national hopes.

According to Christian historians, he did his best to obliterate the sites Christians revered too: he piled dirt over the Holy Sepulchre, for example, and built a pagan temple there. Thus, he accidentally preserved the Holy Sepulchre for the Christian archaeologists of two centuries later.

From our point of view, it seems as if Hadrian's colony was an utter failure. No one but historians even remembers that there was an Aelia Capitolina: Jerusalem is the name of the place now, as it was before Hadrian tried and failed to obliterate its memory.

But the city we see today is very much Hadrian's city. Its street plan comes from Hadrian, who had it laid out in the usual form of a Roman *colonia*, with main streets running east-west and north-south, intersecting at the center. The Temple Mount remains from Solomon's time, and some of Herod's great stones are still there, but the layout of the streets is Hadrian's.

It was Constantine, the first Christian emperor, who began the resurrection of Jerusalem as Jerusalem. His mother, Helena, started a fad for religious pilgrimages to the holy places associated with Christ, and she financed an expedition that dug past Hadrian's pagan temple to the Holy Sepulchre. After that, the city was the most important center of pilgrimage for Christians.

But it was never the most important center of Christian thought. Rome, Alexandria, and Antioch had developed into the centers of Church authority and teaching, as we'll soon see.

42

Still Jerusalem

The rest of the history of Jerusalem is full of drastic changes, yet somehow the city remains what it is. Conquered by Muslims, it remained a majority-Christian city for centuries. Christians conquered it in the Crusades and massacred Muslims. Muslims conquered it and massacred Christians. Everybody massacred the Jews.

Today it's still contested, a place claimed by two different states and three different religions. Yet it's also a place where life moves so slowly that much of the merchandise still comes into the center of the city on donkeys.

Much of that merchandise is trinkets and doodads to be sold to Christian tourists from all over the world. Just as in Constantine's time, tourism is big business in Jerusalem. Christian pilgrims come from all over the world to see where Jesus taught, suffered, died, and rose from the dead.

They aren't seeing the same city. Jerusalem has been destroyed and rebuilt several times since Jesus knew it.

But in another sense, Jerusalem is always the same. It's the pattern for the Jerusalem all of us will know sooner or later: "I [John] saw the holy city, new Jerusalem, coming down out of heaven from God, prepared as a bride adorned for her husband; and I heard a great voice from the throne saying, 'Behold, the dwelling of God is with men. He will dwell with them, and they shall be his people, and God himself will be with them; he will wipe away every tear from their eyes, and death shall be no more, neither shall there be mourning nor crying nor pain any more, for the former things have passed away'" (Rev 21:2–4).

2

Antioch

Let's imagine we're travelers from some far-off land coming to see Antioch for the first time. We've been walking the weary road southward for a long time, and we didn't make it before dark. But as we approach from the hills of the north, luxurious suburban villas line the road, and we make our way from one pool of light to the next.

And then we see it—bright stripes of light spread out below us. We've heard stories of the lights of the big city, but we thought they must be exaggerated. They weren't. Every street is lined with lights, and the walls blaze with illuminations.

As we come in through the city gate, we can't help admiring the titanic walls—more ornamental than useful, as it would turn out, but definitely calculated to be impressive.

And then the bustle inside! People rushing here and there, laughing, gossiping, shopping, as if it were the middle of the day! Most of them are speaking Greek, but it doesn't take long for us to hear a group speaking in our own language. We make our way over and politely introduce ourselves.

"Have we come in the middle of a festival?" we ask.

"No," our new friends tell us, "Antioch is always like this."

And they eagerly fill us in on the wonders of the city—the streetlights (they're very proud of the public street lighting), the colonnades that line the main streets and keep shoppers cool in the midday sun and dry in the rain, the Great Church[1] donated by Constantine himself, the palaces, the theater, the hippodrome.

"But if you really want to go home with a memory for a lifetime," they conclude, "come to the Great Church on Sunday morning and hear that young fellow John preach. That's an experience you'll never forget. There's a reason they call him the man with the golden mouth."

A Greek City in the East

Antioch was founded about three hundred years before Christ by one of Alexander the Great's generals. The Macedonian Alexander had conquered the world—which is to say, most of the places the Greeks knew or cared about. But he died at the age of thirty-two, and his vast empire immediately fell apart. His best generals each seized as much as they could get their hands on, and the one who ended up with Syria and the surrounding area was Seleucus. When he had time to take a break from fighting everybody else, he founded a new capital city and named it for his father, Antiochus.

Syria was a Semitic country, but Antioch became populated by Greek-speaking residents brought in by Seleucus, and it would remain a Greek-speaking city for many centuries. It soon became a famous center of Greek culture. Its religion, too, was Greek, and it filled up with temples to the pagan Greek gods.

---

[1] The Great Church, also known as the Golden House, was Antioch's cathedral, the seat of authority for its patriarch. Construction began in A.D. 327.

The most famous shrine in Antioch, and one of the most famous in the pagan world, was out in a suburb named Daphne and was sacred to Apollo. It was a beautiful place, with a spring burbling through the woods, and in the middle of the sacred grove a temple with a famous oracle, where people would go to ask vital questions and come out with obscure, hard-to-interpret answers that left the god a lot of wiggle room no matter which way events turned out.

Well into Christian times, the Daphne oracle kept a powerful position in the pagan cult. In the reign of Constantine's son Constantius, the Caesar Gallus turned off the oracle by moving the body of a martyr to a shrine at Daphne; martyrs' remains were sacred to Christians, but the pagan gods thought they were icky dead bodies, and Apollo refused to speak.

Jewish Antioch

So Antioch was a big Greek city in the middle of a Syrian country. Nevertheless, though the Greek speakers were the majority and Greek culture was dominant, Antioch had all kinds of people from the beginning, because Seleucus had been very generous with his citizenship policies.

One big group that came in right at the beginning was the Jewish population.

Seleucus had won his kingdom with the help of Jewish mercenaries, and he encouraged some of them to settle in the new capital. From the beginning, according to Josephus, they were full citizens—as much so as the Greeks Seleucus brought in to make the city an outpost of Greek civilization.

By the time of Christ, the Jewish quarter in Antioch was large and prosperous. Herod the Great, with his usual taste for extravagant building, gave the Jewish quarter a beautiful stone-paved shopping street with colonnades down both sides.[2] Antioch was outside his dominion, but Herod's gift sent the strong message that he was the benevolent leader of the whole Jewish world. It may also have indicated a more cynical calculation: that the Jews of Antioch were rich and important enough that he needed to keep on their good side.

This isn't to say life was always easy for the Jews. There were times when ethnic hatreds flared up, as they've done all through history. In the Jewish War that destroyed Jerusalem, the Jews all over the Roman Empire were suspected, just as many Americans not of Japanese ancestry suspected their Japanese neighbors during the Second World War. Ugly violence broke out more than once. But for most of the history of ancient Antioch, the Jewish community remained large and important, even well into Christian times.

It was influential enough that many Greeks in Antioch were attracted to the Jewish religion. They became proselytes—the "God-fearers", as they were called, who had not yet become fully Jewish but came to the synagogues and heard the Scriptures.

Jews everywhere kept in close touch with Jerusalem, but it seems the Jews in Antioch were particularly close to the holy city. They heard news and saw visitors from Jerusalem every day—and vice versa. Luke tells us in Acts 6:5 that the deacon Nicolaus was a proselyte from Antioch. He also tells us that when Jesus' disciples in Jerusalem were scattered after the martyrdom of Stephen, Antioch was one of the places they went. At first they had been preaching

[2] Josephus, *Jewish War* 1.425, trans. H. St. J. Thackeray, M.A., in *Josephus*, vol. 2, *The Jewish War, Books I–III* (Cambridge: Harvard University Press; London: William Heinemann, 1926), p. 201.

only to Jews, but in Antioch they started preaching to non-Jews as well. Paul and Barnabas spent a year teaching in Antioch, and it seems they were so successful in making converts that Antiochenes needed a word to describe *those* people. Luke tells us, "In Antioch the disciples were for the first time called Christians" (11:26).

It was these new Gentile Christians of Antioch who were the subject of the Council of Jerusalem, where it was decided that Gentile Christians would not have to keep the Jewish law (see 15:1–21).

For the next five centuries, Antioch would be one of the most important centers of Christian thought, and as we'll see, it developed its own style of thinking about Christianity. From the beginning, the Christian thinkers of Antioch would focus on the literal sense of Scripture. That would lead some of them to become some of the greatest Christian teachers who ever lived. It would lead others to found some of the most persistent and dangerous heresies.

Saint Ignatius of Antioch

The first great name that comes up among the Christian leaders from Antioch is Saint Ignatius of Antioch. In the early 100s—a time when there were still many people alive who had known the Apostles—he was sent off to martyrdom in Rome, and along the way, he wrote a series of letters to encourage Christians in other churches. The letters are inspiring and instructive, and one of the things they teach us is how important the Church in Antioch had already become. Ignatius writes politely to all the churches, but he writes as if he had a right to teach them something. Only to the Church in Rome does he write as if he were deferring to a superior, calling her "worthy of honor, worthy of the highest happiness, worthy of praise, worthy of obtaining her every desire, worthy of being deemed holy, and which presides over love, is named from Christ, and from the Father".[3]

From Ignatius we learn that the organization of the Church was already well established in Antioch, and he expected congregations in other cities to follow the same structure, as he tells the congregation in Magnesia: "Just as the Lord did nothing without the Father, being united to him, neither by himself nor by the apostles, so neither should you do anything without the bishop and presbyters."[4]

Living in harmony with the bishop is living the way of Christ, as he tells the Trallians. The arrangement of bishop, priests, and deacons is not just a human organization but the way to salvation:

> Since you are subject to the bishop as to Jesus Christ, it seems to me that you are living not after the manner of men, but according to Jesus Christ, who died for us, in order, by believing in his death, you may escape from death. It is therefore necessary—and this is exactly what you are doing—that you should do nothing without the bishop. And you should also be subject to the presbytery, as to the apostle of Jesus Christ, who is our hope, in whom, if we live, we shall be found. It is fitting also that the deacons, who belong to the mysteries of Jesus Christ, should in every respect be pleasing to all. For

---

[3] Ignatius of Antioch, *Letter to the Romans*, salutation, trans. Alexander Roberts and James Donaldson, in *Ante-Nicene Fathers*, vol. 1, ed. Alexander Roberts, James Donaldson, and A. Cleveland Coxe (Buffalo, N.Y.: Christian Literature Publishing, 1885), revised and edited for New Advent by Kevin Knight, https://www.newadvent.org/fathers/0107.htm. Hereafter, *Ante-Nicene Fathers* is cited as *ANF*. Some sources from NewAdvent.org have been adapted to modern English.

[4] Ignatius of Antioch, *Letter to the Magnesians* 7, short version, trans. Roberts and Donaldson, in *ANF*, vol. 1, http://www.newadvent.org/fathers/0105.htm.

they are not ministers of meat and drink, but servants
of the Church of God.[5]

Ignatius of Antioch makes it clear that the bishops of
Antioch were already powerful and influential in the
Church. The next big name in Antioch is Theophilus,
bishop of Antioch in about 170, who wrote a defense
of Christianity against the pagans, a work that still survives. Christianity was a big deal in Antioch even before
the emperor Constantine made the Christian religion legal
in the year 313.

As the Church grew, many Christians—men and
women—decided to devote themselves completely to the
Lord. Many of those retreated from the distractions and
temptations of the city and went out into the wilderness.
By the 300s, there were so many of them that they formed
a second city of their own on Mount Silpius outside the
city—one that looked more like a military camp than
the sophisticated urban metropolis they had left. Saint
John Chrysostom describes a desert full of monks' huts
laid out one after another, with the monks leading simple
but worry-free lives.[6] Considering the cares of the big city,
the ascetic life in the hills had a strong appeal:

> They have no reason to be gloomy when evening has over-
> taken them, as many men feel, worrying over the anxious
> thoughts that spring from the evils of the day. After their
> supper, they have no reason to be careful about robbers,

[5] Ignatius of Antioch, *Letter to the Trallians* 2, short version, trans. Roberts and
Donaldson, in *ANF*, vol. 1, https://www.newadvent.org/fathers/0106.htm.

[6] John Chrysostom, *Homily 69 on Matthew* 3–4, trans. George Prevost, revised by M. B. Riddle, in *Nicene and Post-Nicene Fathers*, 1st series, vol. 10, ed.
Philip Schaff (Buffalo, N.Y.: Christian Literature Publishing, 1888), revised
and edited for New Advent by Kevin Knight, https://www.newadvent.org
/fathers/200169.htm. Hereafter, *Nicene and Post-Nicene Fathers* is cited as *NPNF*.

and to shut the doors, and to put bars against them. Nor do they have to dread the other ills of which many are afraid, extinguishing their candles with strict care for fear that a spark anywhere should set the house on fire.[7]

Robbers and fires—two of the biggest worries of life in the big city. And even when you're not worrying about those, you have a thousand other things to worry about. As it turned out, one of those things was the state of the Church herself.

Trouble in the Church

The Church in Antioch was often in turmoil, and more than once it had multiple bishops all claiming to be the only legitimate bishop. The school of Antioch also gave birth to more than one notorious heresy. That same Theophilus whose defense of Christianity still survives wrote several works that haven't survived, and most of them were arguing against one heresy or another.

Not every bishop of Antioch was on the right side of the heresy line. Paul of Samosata was a bishop of Antioch who began teaching a radical interpretation of the Incarnation. According to him, Jesus was just a man who was really, really good. The Word of God, meanwhile, was never separated from God. Jesus was inspired by the Word but was not the Word himself.

What made Paul's heresy so dangerous was that he was a great entertainer. He preached homilies that had the crowds cheering and clapping. This was normal practice, by the way: Christians applauded their preachers the way

[7] Ibid., 4.

they would applaud orators in the forum or actors on the stage, in spite of many Christian preachers who told them it was unseemly behavior. And Paul was really good at getting applause. He demanded it, in fact: "He rebukes and insults those who do not applaud and wave their handkerchiefs as they do in the theaters, and shout and leap about like the men and women that are stationed around him", other bishops complained.[8] Ultimately, he was condemned as a heretic by the rest of the Church, but he would not be the last bishop of Antioch who would lead people down the wrong path. And he gives us a clue that may help us understand why heresies were so attractive and why the battles over them were so vicious. They weren't just philosophical debates. These preachers were the rap stars of their age. They were celebrities with big fan bases.

The biggest heresy of them all started in Antioch. Arius had come to Antioch to study with Saint Lucian, one of the best-known Christian teachers there. It was after he returned to Alexandria in Egypt that he began teaching his doctrine that the Son of God was a created being, not coeternal with the Father. So although the Arian heresy really belongs more to Alexandria, the germ of it came from Antioch.

In 313, the emperor Constantine finally made Christianity legal. As we know, the Church didn't live happily ever after. Instead, with the Church becoming a route to power and influence, the question of which doctrine was the right one and who was the right bishop became much more hotly contested.

---

[8] Eusebius, *Church History* 7.30.9, trans. Arthur Cushman McGiffert, in *NPNF*, 2nd series, vol. 1, ed. Philip Schaff and Henry Wace (Buffalo, N.Y.: Christian Literature Publishing, 1890), revised and edited for New Advent by Kevin Knight, https://www.newadvent.org/fathers/250107.htm.

And the pagans had not conceded defeat. That was important, because in 361, one of Constantine's nephews, Julian, became emperor and suddenly announced he was a pagan. Future historians would call him Julian the Apostate.

Paganism Claws Its Way Back

Immediately, Julian started trying to undo Christianity. And in 363, the news came in: he was coming to make his headquarters at Antioch.

Why Antioch?

First of all, it wasn't Constantinople. That was important. Constantinople had been a Christian city since Constantine elevated it from provincial town to imperial capital. It was built to be Christian. Antioch, on the other hand, was centuries old, and it had strong pagan traditions.

It was also the home of Libanius, the most admired literary figure among the remaining pagans and the most distinguished professor of rhetoric in the whole empire. Julian counted Libanius as a personal friend. Libanius would give the pagan revival its intellectual foundation—something that was terribly important to an emperor who thought of himself as one of the leading intellectuals of his age.

And then there was the practical consideration that Julian had his eye on Persia. Of the four great centers of culture in the Roman Empire, Antioch was the obvious choice for launching an expedition against the rival empire in the East.

So Julian came to Antioch with high hopes of making it the capital of his new Hellenism.

He was doomed to disappointment.

The citizens of Antioch didn't take him seriously. They laughed at his beard. Julian was very vain about his beard, and they laughed at it. It made him look like some pretentious philosopher. Well, yes, looking like a philosopher was the point of having a beard. But they *laughed* at it.

Julian had been painting pictures in his mind of parades and huge celebrations when he went to the temple of Apollo at Daphne for the annual festival of the god. Instead, he found one priest with a goose he had brought from home to sacrifice. This was supposed to be one of the most famous pagan festivals in the Roman world! Where was everybody?

And then, not long afterward, the temple of Apollo caught fire and burned. Julian blamed the Christians, of course. The cathedral in Antioch was closed, and Julian's minions confiscated the treasures that had been donated by Constantine.

Julian left Antioch in a sour mood. Then he was killed in Persia, so it didn't much matter how he felt about Antioch.

What Julian had discovered was that it was too late for Antioch—too late to make it into a pagan capital. Antioch was Christian. There were still pagans in the city, but they were irrelevant. Even the famous rhetorical school of the belligerently pagan Libanius was turning out the next generation of great Christian thinkers.

The Man with the Golden Mouth

Of all the Christian thinkers who came out of Antioch, the most famous by far is Saint John Chrysostom—John the Golden-Mouthed.

John was born in about 347 into a Christian world, but it was a world where paganism was still strong and—as the reign of Julian showed—still held out hopes of reconquering the Roman Empire. John was a teenager when Julian was emperor; he would have carried a strong memory of those dark years for the rest of his life.

John had a lot of variety in his life. He was raised by a single mother, who fortunately had money—though she had to fight off scheming relatives to keep it. She was able to pay for the best education money could buy, so John ended up in the rhetorical school of Libanius, where he was the star pupil. But John had been raised a Christian, and his Christian faith pulled him more and more toward the Church. He gave up his ambition and joined the ascetics in the desert. He pushed his asceticism so hard, though, that he ruined his health, and he had to go back to the city to recover.

Ordained as a priest by Meletius, one of the claimants to the see of Antioch, John began preaching, and right away he was a star. All that stuff he had learned from Libanius worked just as well in a Christian homily as it did in a classical oration. The crowds went wild—and crowds in Antioch were just as enthusiastic in the church as they were in the theater. They clapped and cheered. They laughed at the jokes. John halfheartedly told them they should sit quietly and listen, but when he said that, they clapped and cheered even more. And John loved it, as he confessed.

Theologically, John was in the tradition of the school of Antioch. He emphasized the literal meaning of Scripture and how it applies to the way we live our lives. Because of that emphasis, we learn a lot about daily life in Antioch in the late 300s from John. It was a city of striking contrasts: drunken revelry in the streets, but also three thousand women who had decided to become consecrated virgins; rowdy mobs at the horse races, as well as standing-room-only crowds in church when John was preaching. It was a majority-Christian city, but it was also a place where Jewish and pagan communities were still large and powerful.

Christians had learned a lot from the Jews in Antioch, and the two communities were closely related. When we read Church Fathers in Antioch warning their flock against adopting Jewish customs and going to Jewish feasts, it's clear they're worried precisely because there wasn't a sharp line drawn between Christian and Jew. "But the Jewish rituals are so impressive", the Christians responded. "Why shouldn't we celebrate together when the differences between us are so small?" Church leaders like John worried that such Christians would be led away into the splinter groups who insisted that Christians had to keep the Jewish law.

Clearly the Jews of Antioch were still a large and influential group when John was writing. So were the pagans. John had lived through the reign of Julian. When he was a young man, he had seen with his own eyes how close the Christian revolution came to being undone. Pagan power was real, and it was disproportionately influential. We know from history that the pagans were on the losing side and that they were destined to fade away over the next two centuries. But the Christians of the middle 300s didn't have our advantage. Their fear of paganism was genuine, and it was understandable.

John saw Christians celebrating the new year with their pagan neighbors, and it worried him. The forum was splendidly decorated, and all the shopkeepers had their shiniest wares on display. And, of course, everybody was drunk. It was a superstition that you had to be riotously joyful as the new year came in to make good fortune for the rest of the year. Preaching to his congregation, John reminded them they were at war and the demons were the enemy: "The diabolical night-festivities that occur today, the jests, the abuse, and the nocturnal dances, and this comedy, absurd and worse than every enemy, took our city captive."[9]

[9] John Chrysostom, "In Kalendas—On the Kalends of January", trans. Seumas Macdonald, Tertullian.org, commissioned by Roger Pearse, 2010, https://www.tertullian.org/fathers/chrysostom_in_kalendas.htm. Some sources from Tertullian.org have been adapted to modern English.

The Church was important and well developed in Antioch by John's time. John describes how it had hospitals and homes for the aged and hostels for travelers. Much of what would be done by the government today was done by the Church. There was even a time when the Church managed to save the city from complete annihilation.

The Statues

It started when the emperor Theodosius imposed new taxes that seemed burdensome to the mob in Antioch. A riot followed. Now, riots were common in ancient cities, and they were immediately forgiven and forgotten most of the time. But this time the rioters got carried away and pulled down the statues of the emperor and his family, dragging them through the streets like criminals.

That was going too far. The statues were the imperial family's presence in the city. This was treason.

Roman cities were left to govern themselves for the most part, but this independence meant that the whole city was responsible when something bad happened. And Theodosius had a notorious temper. When the people sobered up, they realized they were in trouble—the kind of trouble that could lead to a massacre of thousands and the whole city being leveled.

In those dark days, John preached a series of sermons that were never forgotten by those who heard them. He didn't conceal how bad the situation was. But he somehow gave the people hope.

John describes what the city was like: "Once our city was the happiest place on earth. Now there's nowhere so sad. The people used to buzz around the forum like bees around their hive, and everyone said how lucky we were that there were so many of us. Now look at us! The hive is deserted! Fear has chased us away, like smoke chasing bees."[10]

No one was in the forum, he said. Where there had been a constant river of people, one or two forlorn figures were hurrying through with their heads down. Free men sat inside shackled with their slaves. Whenever they thought they could talk to someone safely, they asked, "Who got taken away today? Who's been arrested? Who's been killed? How did it go? What happened?"

The story had a happy ending. The bishop of Antioch himself successfully pleaded with Theodosius to spare the city. But no one ever forgot those dark days—and the sermons that made John famous across the Roman Empire.

In fact, they made him too famous. He was chosen as bishop of Constantinople, the imperial capital, based on the fame he had earned in Antioch. In Constantinople, he had a miserable time, and he ultimately died in exile.

Nestorius and the Decline of Antioch

Antioch, meanwhile, was not through turning out famous theologians. John Chrysostom's friend Theodore of Mopsuestia wrote important works still read today, but his reputation in later centuries had some serious ups and downs. Stories associated him with a younger theologian who was destined to be much more influential: Nestorius.

Nestorius was trained in Antioch, and he was respected for his learning—so much so that he was made bishop of Constantinople in 428.

[10]John Chrysostom, *Homily 2 on the Statues* 3, trans. W. R. W. Stephens, in *NPNF*, 1st series, vol. 9, ed. Philip Schaff (Buffalo, N.Y.: Christian Literature Publishing, 1889), revised and edited for New Advent by Kevin Knight, http://www.newadvent.org/fathers/190102.htm.

That was when things started to go wrong for him.

Nestorius told his flock they shouldn't call Mary "Mother of God". She was Mother of the Christ, but she was mother of Jesus' human nature only.

This separation of the natures did not go over well. It provoked a big battle in the Church, and under the leadership of Cyril of Alexandria, Nestorius was condemned at the Council of Ephesus in 431. He retired to a monastery in Antioch but was eventually exiled to a place called Oasis in Egypt.

Many Christians in the East, including in Antioch, never accepted the condemnation of Nestorius. To this day, he is considered a saint in several Eastern Christian traditions.

Partly because of these ongoing disputes, Antioch began to lose some of its influence in the larger Church. But the city was still the great metropolis of the East in the year 500. Then, in 525, a huge fire hit the city.

Fires were common in ancient cities. This one was mild by comparison to some: it wrecked the center of the city, but it looked as though the city would recover.

But only a few months later, a titanic earthquake reduced much of the city to rubble. It happened when most people were inside at dinner. Historians say that a a quarter of a million people died. Fires broke out. Looting followed.

The city had just begun to recover when, two and a half years later, another earthquake shook it to pieces, flattening what was left. Once again the city started to rebuild, though archaeologists say it was on a much smaller scale. But then in 540, the Persian army took the city and burned it to the ground, with the usual pillage and massacres. And then two years later came the plague. And then came more earthquakes. And the Persians came back and burned the place again.

There was little left of Antioch by the time the conquering Arabs came in. Antioch surrendered easily, partly because it had no way of defending itself, and partly because the Arabs made surrendering easy—just pay your tax and get on with your lives, and we'll leave you alone. The population remained mostly Christian for centuries, and the city was eventually conquered by Western European Christians in the Crusades. Today it's a medium-sized city in the southeastern corner of Turkey, with little left above ground to show that it was once the leading city of the East.

Today there are several patriarchs of Antioch: the patriarch of Antioch who leads the Syriac Orthodox Church and lives in Damascus; a Melkite patriarch of Antioch, also in Damascus; a Greek Orthodox patriarch of Antioch, again in Damascus; a Maronite patriarch of Antioch in Bkerké, the see of Lebanon; and a Syriac Catholic patriarch of Antioch in Beirut.

There are no patriarchs of Antioch in Antioch.

3

Rome

They call Rome the Eternal City. It's always changing and always the same. It's home to ancient temples and modern skyscrapers. It's the capital of one of the great nations of modern times, but every street and alley preserves memories of the time when it was the capital of the world. Turn a corner, and the Colosseum looms ahead, impossibly huge even in its broken splendor. Turn another corner, and there's Trajan's Column, with its pictorial record of the conquest of far-off Dacia—today's Romania, which still preserves the name of its Roman conquerors more than nineteen hundred years later.

And right across the street from Trajan's Column are two churches with magnificent domes, almost right next to each other. Because in a way this is still the capital of the world. Rome is the seat of the Catholic Church, the biggest religious organization on earth. Wherever you are on the globe, Rome still has authority. But now it's an authority that doesn't depend on legions with spears. It's the authority Christ gave to Peter, the Apostle his friends would have voted Least Likely to Succeed.

From Village to Megalopolis

No one would have guessed when Rome was founded that it would become anything important. Antioch was built to be a capital city from the beginning. Rome was just a village in the hills along the Tiber River. Legend says it was founded in 753 B.C. by Romulus and Remus, twin brothers who were descended from Trojans who fled after the Greek army destroyed Troy. For a long time, it was governed by kings from Rome's much more powerful neighbors, the Etruscans. Then the Romans threw out their Etruscan masters and governed themselves as a republic. As a republic, they conquered the whole Mediterranean world, but all that conquering bred strong military leaders who were impatient with laws and formalities. A few years before the birth of Christ, after a long series of civil wars, Augustus made himself emperor—the head man in charge of the whole Roman government. From then on, the Roman world was governed by emperors. They kept all the old institutions of the republic; they just made sure those institutions didn't have any power to stand in their way.

By the time of Augustus, Rome was the biggest city in the world. It had a million people crowded into narrow streets of high-rise tenements—more than forty thousand apartment buildings, according to one count.[1] And since it was the city that ruled the whole world—or at least all the parts of the world that were important to the Romans—it attracted all kinds of people from all over. The Latin-speaking Romans often complained about all the strange people with strange customs who were taking up residence in their city, but when you conquer the world, you have to expect a few immigrants.

---

[1] Tertius Chandler, *Four Thousand Years of Urban Growth: An Historical Census* (Lewiston, N.Y.: St. David's University Press, 1987), pp. 95, 97; Ivana Della Portella, *Subterranean Rome* (Cologne: Könemann, 2000), p. 217. A million people is a common estimate, but some historians make the number half that. Almost all agree, though, that Rome was the largest city in the world at the time of Christ.

One of the groups they complained about most often was the Jews.

Jewish Rome

By the time of Christ, there was a large Jewish population in Rome. It was large enough that the xenophobic Romans were worried about it: these were people who spoke Greek,[2] had strange customs, and dressed differently. The famous Roman orator Cicero (who died forty-three years before Christ) gives us a good picture of Roman feelings about the Jews in his defense of Flaccus, a Roman governor accused of stealing the Temple contribution raised in his province. Jews all over the world paid a tax to the Temple in Jerusalem, but Flaccus made it illegal to export gold from his province and confiscated all the money. In defending him against the charges brought against him, Cicero played on the Romans' suspicion of these foreigners in their midst:

> You know how numerous that crowd is, how great is its unanimity, and of what weight it is in the popular assemblies. I will speak in a low voice, just so as to let the judges hear me. For men are not wanting who would be glad to excite that people against me and against every eminent man; and I will not assist them and enable them to do so more easily.[3]

According to Cicero, Jews formed mobs who disrupted the popular assemblies. (A Jewish resident might point out that the popular assemblies had never been models of

[2] Harry J. Leon, *The Jews of Ancient Rome* (Philadelphia: Jewish Publication Society of America, 1960), p. 75.

[3] Cicero, *For L. Flaccus* 28, in *The Orations of Marcus Tullius Cicero*, vol. 2, trans. C. D. Yonge (London: Henry G. Bohn, 1852), p. 454.

decorum and frequently devolved into riots.) And their religion was weird.

But to resist the barbarous superstition of the Jews would be an act of dignity. To despise the mob of Jews, which was sometimes very unruly in the assemblies, in defense of the interests of the republic, was an act of the greatest wisdom.[4]

How weird was that religion? As weird as the popular imagination could make it. Romans knew that the Jews had very different customs, but few of them knew exactly what those customs were. The question of why Jews refused to eat pork was fascinating to them. Some deduced that the Jews worshiped pigs.[5] The Jewish Sabbath was also a notable thing—a regularly recurring day of rest, but what did Jews do when they weren't working? Some said they fasted. Some said they worshiped one of the forms of Jupiter. Now, of course, any Roman could have gone to a Jewish neighbor and asked, but educated Romans wouldn't do that. Instead, they would pore over the most famous Greek writers and try to find some hint there about where the Jews had come from (probably Crete, said the old writers) and what their customs were.

So this was what average Romans thought about Jews: there were a lot of them, they spoke Greek, they had weird customs that might be dangerous, and they all acted together as if they were in on some sort of conspiracy. Obviously, this was mostly ignorant xenophobia, but ignorant xenophobia was how Roman leaders made their decisions. Flaccus was acquitted; the Roman judges agreed with Cicero that he was perfectly right to confiscate the Jews' Temple contributions.

So we know that Rome had a large Jewish population, and that would have given the first Christians a familiar

[4] Ibid.
[5] Leon, *Jews of Ancient Rome*, p. 38.

base of operations. The earliest Christians started in the Jewish community wherever they went, and in Rome, a Latin-speaking city, the Jews were a group who spoke the familiar Greek of the eastern half of the empire.

Saint Peter and the Roman Church

We don't know who the first Christians were in Rome. They might have been sailors or soldiers or merchants— ordinary people who had heard the Good News and brought it with them as they traveled.

By the time Saint Paul was writing his longest letter (Romans), there was already a large congregation in Rome—and Paul hadn't been there yet. Peter wasn't there at the time, either, or Paul would not have addressed the congregation in such commanding tones, and he certainly wouldn't have left Cephas out of the long list of personal greetings at the end. Paul and Peter sometimes had their differences, but Paul would never have just ignored Peter.

It's not surprising that there was already a Church at Rome. Rome was the biggest city in the world, and everyone who traveled got there eventually. Not only was it the top destination in its own right, but it was on the way from everywhere in the East to everywhere in the West.

When Peter arrived in Rome, he took over the leadership of the Church there. Scripture doesn't tell us when he got there—the Acts of the Apostles ends with Paul still on his way to Rome and Peter not there yet. But tradition and later writers are so universally agreed that Peter was the first leader of the Christian Church in Rome that no serious historian can doubt it.

Its position in the capital would have made the Roman Church important, but having Peter as its bishop (a word that comes from the Greek for "overseer") made Rome the leading Church in the world. "On this rock I will build my Church" (Mt 16:18), Christ had told Peter, and it was Peter he told to "feed my sheep" after the Resurrection (Jn 21:17).

Peter and his flock knew he could not live forever on earth. Would the end of the world come before he died? No, but the end of Rome nearly did.

The Persecution

In the year 64, a fire started in Rome that spread out of control and burned for nine days. When it finally burned out, more than half the city was in ashes.

The emperor Nero immediately started building an extravagant palace on the ruins, which led to common gossip that Nero had started the fire to clear the land he coveted. Looking around for a scapegoat, Nero hit on the new and weird sect of the Christians. They were a kind of Jews, and Jews were always good for blaming things on. But they had become distinct enough that people knew who they were and believed all kinds of strange rumors about them. They thought the end of the world was near, didn't they? They probably started the fire to bring the end of the world closer.

That was the story Nero wanted people to have in their minds, anyway. He started rounding up the Christians and torturing them to death for the entertainment of the Roman people. The Roman people liked it. They wanted more.

Peter and Paul were among the martyrs. Tradition says that Peter was crucified upside down, at his own request, because he thought he was not worthy to die the same death as his Lord. Paul was a Roman citizen, and Roman citizens could not be crucified, so he was beheaded instead.

Nero's persecution established a precedent. Until then, there had been no official Roman policy about the Christians. But now it was officially illegal to be a Christian, and the penalty was death.

That was the grim background against which the Church started growing explosively. A Christian might be taken and sent to die at any time. And Christians' deaths were popular entertainment. That massive Colosseum that still looms in Rome, still the biggest amphitheater in the world, was often filled to capacity with crowds who had come to enjoy the spectacle of Christians being torn apart by wild animals. This was the average Roman's idea of fun.

But these martyrdoms didn't discourage the Christians. In fact, they just made more Christians. Every year, more ordinary Romans saw that these Christians were confident enough to face the worst kind of death for what they believed in, and those ordinary Romans said, "Well, there must be something in it." Every year, the Church in Rome—and all over the world—grew bigger.

The Chair of Peter

And as the Church all over the Roman world grew, she looked to Peter's successors as her leaders.

Saint Clement of Rome is one of the earliest Christian writers outside the Bible. According to the most common tradition, he was the fourth bishop of Rome, after Peter, Linus, and Anacletus. Clement himself had been a disciple of Peter.

So when Clement acts as though he has authority over the other churches, it's fair to assume he takes that authority from Peter. Clement's letter to the Church in Corinth is addressing some of the same problems that Saint Paul's two letters to the Corinthians addressed: the Corinthian

Church was full of bickering factions, and one faction had tossed out some leaders who Clement thought ought to be reinstated.

For us, what's important about the letter is that Clement assumes he has the authority to tell the Corinthians to knock it off. He begins with a salutation that treats the Corinthian Church as a fellow congregation: "The Church of God which sojourns at Rome, to the Church of God sojourning at Corinth ..."[6] But after some complimentary phrases designed to put his correspondents in a receptive mood, he starts telling the Corinthians what to do. He doesn't say "In my opinion" or "If I were in your place". He simply tells them, by the authority of the Holy Spirit, what needs to be done.

Not that he himself is perfect. He reminds them that he is a sinner too, and so are all the Christians in the Church at Rome. "We write these things to you, beloved, not just to admonish you of your duty, but also to remind ourselves. For we are struggling on the same arena, and the same conflict is assigned to both of us."[7] Nevertheless, it's his job to admonish the Corinthians.

In the other direction, we already saw how Saint Ignatius of Antioch deferred to the Roman Church—"the church that presides over the brotherhood of love", as he called it[8]—though he assumed the authority to teach and correct all the other churches he wrote to.

[6] Clement, *First Letter of Clement* 1, trans. John Keith, in *ANF*, vol. 9, ed. Allan Menzies (Buffalo, N.Y.: Christian Literature Publishing, 1896), revised and edited for New Advent by Kevin Knight, https://www.newadvent.org/fathers/1010 .htm. (The *First Letter of Clement* is also known as *Letter to the Corinthians*.)

[7] Ibid., 7.

[8] Ignatius of Antioch, *Letter to the Romans*, preface, trans. Alexander Roberts and James Donaldson, in *ANF*, vol. 1, ed. Alexander Roberts, James Donaldson, and A. Cleveland Coxe (Buffalo, N.Y.: Christian Literature Publishing, 1885), revised and edited for New Advent by Kevin Knight, https://www .newadvent.org/fathers/0107.htm.

In the very earliest days of the Church, the most important Christian figures were already assuming that the Church at Rome was the leader of all the churches, and that its bishop had the authority to decide on questions of faith and discipline. Throughout the age of the Fathers, this faith didn't waver. In the middle 200s, for example, Saint Dionysius, bishop of Alexandria—one of the most important Christian churches—wrote to Pope Sixtus II to ask about the validity of heretical baptism. "For truly, brother, I am in need of counsel, and I ask your judgment concerning a certain matter which has come to me, fearing that I may be in error."[9] Pope Sixtus is not remembered as one of the great theologians of all time, but he had the authority of Peter, and that was what Dionysius needed.

This is the strange thing about the Church in Rome. There aren't very many early Church Fathers with "of Rome" after their names. When you mention Clement of Rome and Hippolytus of Rome, you've rattled off the whole list. You might add Pope Dionysius, who was bishop of Rome from 259 to 268 and whose few works are mostly lost. But that's about it. Yet the bishop of Rome was clearly recognized as the leader of the whole Church right from the beginning. When the greatest minds of the ancient Church turned to the bishop of Rome for definitive answers, it was not because he was smarter than they were but because he had the authority.

The clearest statement of Rome's authority came not from a pope but from Saint Irenaeus of Lyons, who wrote an encyclopedia of Christian heresies (*Against Heresies*) not long before the year 200. We'll hear more about him

[9] Dionysius' letter is quoted in Eusebius, *Church History* 7.9.1, trans. Arthur Cushman McGiffert, in *NPNF*, 2nd series, vol. 1, ed. Philip Schaff and Henry Wace (Buffalo, N.Y.: Christian Literature Publishing, 1890), revised and edited for New Advent by Kevin Knight, https://www.newadvent.org/fathers/250107.htm.

when we get to Lugdunum, but it's worth hearing how he explains the way to tell which of the many ideas claiming to be "Christian" is the right one. He points out that anyone can trace the line of bishops in any important city back to the Apostles. But we don't have to do that in every Christian Church. Tracing the Church in Rome back to Peter will be enough. He explains,

> Since, however, it would be very tedious in a book like this to list the successions of all the churches, we'll put to confusion all those who, in whatever manner, whether by an evil self-pleasing, by vainglory, or by blindness and perverse opinion, assemble in unauthorized meetings. All we have to do is point to that tradition derived from the apostles, of the very great, the very ancient, and universally known church founded and organized at Rome by the two most glorious apostles, Peter and Paul. We point to the faith preached to men, which comes down to our time by means of the successions of the bishops. For it is necessary for every church—that is, the faithful everywhere—to agree with this church, on account of its pre-eminent authority.[10]

After this, Irenaeus lists the bishops of Rome: first Peter, then Linus, then Anacletus, and then Clement. He continues, "In the time of this Clement, no small dissension having occurred among the brethren at Corinth, the Church in Rome sent a very powerful letter to the Corinthians, exhorting them to peace, renewing their faith, and declaring the tradition which it had lately received from the apostles."[11]

Irenaeus continues the list down to his own day, and he makes the point very well. You know what Peter and Paul

[10] Irenaeus, *Against Heresies* 3.3.2, trans. Members of the English Church, in *Five Books of S. Irenaeus, Bishop of Lyons, Against Heresies* (Oxford: James Parker, 1872).
[11] Ibid., 3.3.3.

taught. You know what Clement taught, and he still had their voices ringing in his ears. You know that the bishop of Rome still teaches the same things today. You know that Rome has preeminent authority in the Church. Therefore, you know who's right when a heretic starts teaching some new doctrine as if it came straight from Christ. Rome sets the standard, because the bishop of Rome is in a line that goes straight back to the Apostles.

This doesn't mean Irenaeus thought the pope was always right. When Pope Victor excommunicated the churches of Asia for celebrating Easter on a different date, Irenaeus sent him a letter advising him to reconsider and preserve the peace between the churches. He didn't contest Victor's *authority* to make that decision, but he was ready to tell Victor what he thought of it. It's precisely because he recognized Victor as leader of the whole Church that he felt compelled to write the letter he wrote.[12]

So far we've met some of the leaders of the Roman Church and seen what the great minds from elsewhere said about Rome's leadership. But we also know more about the ordinary Christians of Rome than we know about Christians anywhere else, because they left a vivid record of their lives in one of the world's most amazing time capsules.

The Catacombs

One of the gloomy necessities of life in the big city is disposing of citizens who die. The ancient Romans had a superstitious horror of dead bodies, and of course it's also true that corpses can carry infections. For religious and

---

[12] Margherita Guarducci, *The Primacy of the Church of Rome: Documents, Reflections, Proofs* (San Francisco: Ignatius Press, 2003), 23.

sanitary reasons, it was the law that bodies could not be buried within the city walls. Cremation was the general practice of pagan Romans, but Jews and Christians usually buried their dead.

Conveniently, the hills just outside the city were riddled with abandoned quarries that made a good start on an underground tomb complex. And as soon as they started burying their dead in these networks of tunnels, the Christians started decorating them.

At first, the decorations included many pagan elements from traditional Roman culture. Figures from classical mythology often appear in Christian art in the catacombs. These pictures may have been standard patterns that were used by tomb painters for both pagans and Christians. But certainly the Christians adopted them with a different understanding. The pagan themes are repurposed as Christian symbolism.

Partly this is for the same reason that our cemeteries today have such eclectic symbolism. The monument dealers kept stock models on hand. If your relative died suddenly, you would go buy a sarcophagus, and if it was one with a nice hunting scene on it, at least that wasn't offensive to your Christian faith.

But it's also true that some mythology lent itself well to Christian interpretations. The phoenix, the legendary rarest bird in the world, was a good example. There was only one phoenix, and when it grew old, it burst into flames and burned up on its own funeral pyre. Then a new phoenix was born from the ashes. This was a ready-made symbol of Christian resurrection, and the Christians were happy to adopt it.[13]

[13] Fabrizio Bisconti, "The Decoration of Roman Catacombs", in *The Christian Catacombs of Rome: History, Decoration, Inscriptions*, by Vincenzo Fiocchi Nicolai, Fabrizio Bisconti, and Danilo Mazzoleni (Regensburg: Schnell & Steiner, 2002), pp. 100–103.

The myth of Orpheus was also popular in Christian catacomb art. Orpheus famously soothed the animals with
his music; he is often depicted with the attributes of the
Good Shepherd. Orpheus also raided hell to bring back
Eurydice, although that didn't work out perfectly for him.
Orpheus may also represent David, the most famous musi-
cian in Scripture.[14]

People in the catacomb art are often represented with
their arms held out and their hands open to heaven—a
position called the orant, or praying position. This was
a common position of prayer in all religions in ancient
times; it appears in both pagan and Christian art.

The earlier art in the catacombs is more likely to have
non-Christian themes. As Christians became more numer-
ous, and probably wealthier, we see more specifically
Christian decoration.[15] We might analyze this as more
tradesmen and artists becoming Christians or as tradesmen
discovering a large client base and giving the customers
what they wanted. It could be both.

These Christian images show us everything that was
important to the people who were buried in the catacombs, and to the friends and families who survived them.
Sometimes we see Christ, the Apostles, or the martyrs.
The earliest artistic images of Christ that have survived are
in the catacombs—very often as the Good Shepherd carrying a lamb on his shoulders. Images from Old Testament
history are also very popular.

But we also see scenes from ordinary life—things that
would remind visitors to the tomb of what the Christians buried there had done when they were alive. You
can see a greengrocer selling his greens, a barrel maker's

[14] Ibid., p. 103.
[15] Ibid., p. 100.

shop, a shoemaker's tools, bargemen crossing the river.[16] These precious records tell us more about the daily lives of Roman Christians than volumes of theology, no matter how important that theology is. They make those early Christians live again in our imaginations.

Christian Empire

Everything changed for the Christians when Constantine the Great took over the empire in 312. On the eve of the battle for Rome, Constantine had a vision of a cross in the sky with the words "In this sign you shall conquer." He rode into Rome victorious and Christian, and from then on—except during the reign of Julian the Apostate—the emperors were Christian. Not the aristocracy in the city of Rome, though: some of them were Christian, but a large percentage of the senators remained stubbornly pagan for decades.

But the Roman Senate had been mostly irrelevant for a long time, and it was about to become even more irrelevant. Constantine decided to move his imperial capital to the East, picking the small but easily defended Greek city of Byzantium. Calling it "New Rome", he set about building it into a capital city that would eclipse the old Rome in the West. It would soon be known by his own name—Constantinople.

This was the beginning of a long, slow decline in importance for Rome. It was still the biggest city in the world for a long while after that, but the emperors were usually somewhere else. More and more the empire was split into Eastern and Western halves, with the two emperors

[16] Ibid., pp. 118–19.

cooperating or trying to kill each other, depending on their moods. And the emperors in the West more and more ignored Rome, preferring to make their capital at Milan, where they could be closer to the barbarians who needed to be fought, or Ravenna, where they could be as far from the action as possible.

Constantinople was built to be a Christian city from the beginning. Old Rome, on the other hand, had its crusty old traditions. It was the capital of the Catholic Church, but long after the empire had officially become Christian, pagan sacrifices were still offered at Rome and still funded by the government treasury.

This isn't to say Rome was mostly pagan. Constantine and his successors put up lavish Christian churches there. Several of them still stand. They were built on the model of the Roman judgment hall, the basilica. Pagan temples were not places where people gathered for worship services, so they didn't work as models for Christian churches. The judgment hall was a place where a large audience gathered to hear the speeches and watch the judges make their decisions, so it was well adapted to the Christian liturgy. Thus, ordinary Romans went to church every Sunday, but many in the aristocratic minority clung to their pagan ways.

In 395, the emperor Theodosius defeated a usurper and became the sole emperor of the entire Roman Empire. (No one knew it at the time, but he would be the last to control both the Eastern and the Western halves.) Theodosius was a firm Catholic Christian who clamped down on the Arian heresy. He also decided it was about time the last remnants of paganism were stamped out.

The pagan historian Zosimus tells us what happened when Theodosius became sole emperor and confronted the Senate. The Senate had no power over an emperor, but Theodosius still thought it worth his while to try to persuade them. According to Zosimus (who was probably writing more than a hundred years later and relied on now-lost earlier sources), Theodosius made an attempt to evangelize them. It went about as well as you might expect.

The emperor convened the Senate, who firmly adhered to the ancient rites and customs of their country. In an oration, he exhorted them to relinquish their former errors, as he termed them, and to embrace the Christian faith, which promises absolution from all sins and impieties. But not a single individual could be persuaded to abandon the ancient ceremonies, which had been handed down to them from the building of their city, and join with those who felt contempt for the gods. As those in the Senate said, they had lived in the observance of them almost twelve hundred years, in which time their city had never been conquered; therefore, should they change, they could not foresee what might ensue.

Well, if the Senate would not make the decision themselves, Theodosius would make it for them. Theodosius told them that the treasury was exhausted by the expense of sacred rites and sacrifices and that he would therefore abolish them. He did not think them commendable, nor could the army spare so much money. The Senate in reply observed that the sacrifices were not duly performed unless the charges were defrayed from the public funds. Thus, the laws for the performance of sacred rites and sacrifices were repealed and abolished, as well as other institutions and ceremonies that had been received from their ancestors.[17]

Zosimus, being a pagan, tells us that everything went downhill from there, and it was all because the sacrifices to the ancient gods were discontinued. But most historians

---

[17]Johannes Leunclavius Zosimus and Photius, *The New History* 4.60, trans. Anonymous and John Henry Freese (Pittsburgh: Serif Press, 2022).

would say there were other more important reasons. The most important, perhaps, was that Theodosius didn't live much longer. He died at the age of forty-eight and left his sons in charge. The one in the East, Arcadius, was seventeen years old. The one in the West, Honorius, was ten.

The Sack of Rome, and the Sack of Rome, and the Sack of Rome

Historians like to reevaluate previously despised rulers and show how they were actually a lot smarter than people used to think. But it would be hard to find a single historian willing to say that Honorius was a wise and capable ruler. During his reign, the Western Empire lost more territory to the barbarians than in the reign of any other emperor.

To be fair to Honorius, he had to face some very intelligent and formidable barbarian enemies. The most formidable was Alaric, the Gothic leader who wanted to be a Roman general.

Every time the Romans made an agreement with Alaric, Honorius would go back on it. It was exasperating. As barbarians went, Alaric was a very reasonable man. He was certainly more reasonable than Honorius. Even when Alaric had surrounded Rome and was besieging the capital of the world, Honorius wouldn't budge. Holed up in Ravenna, Honorius didn't much care what happened to Rome. Alaric made reasonable requests—make him a Roman general, and he would protect the empire instead of ravaging it. Honorius responded with insults. So Alaric finally turned his soldiers loose on Rome.

Even then, it was a much gentler sacking than most cities got in ancient times. Alaric, who was an Arian Christian, gave his soldiers strict orders that they were just to plunder the city, not to massacre the inhabitants. Citizens could go to the churches for refuge, and the soldiers wouldn't touch them.

Still, it wasn't a good time to be in Rome. Alaric could give his soldiers whatever orders he liked, but a barbarian mob turned loose on the richest city in the world wasn't going to be careful about breaking things.

Saint Jerome was in Palestine when he heard the news. He reacted with the same shock and horror that overcame almost everyone else in the empire. If this could happen in Rome, who was safe? "My voice sticks in my throat; and, as I dictate, sobs choke my utterance. The City which had taken the whole world was itself taken; nay more famine was beforehand with the sword and but few citizens were left to be made captives. In their frenzy the starving people had recourse to hideous food; and tore each other limb from limb that they might have flesh to eat. Even the mother did not spare the babe at her breast."[18]

Jerome then quotes Virgil's *Aeneid*:

> What tongue can tell the slaughter of that night?
> What eyes can weep the sorrows and affright?
> An ancient and imperial city falls;
> The streets are fill'd with frequent funerals ...
> All parts resound with tumults, plaints, and fears;
> And grisly death in sundry shapes appears.[19]

Jerome wrote these words in a letter to Principia, one of his close female friends in Rome. He recalls the story he heard of what happened when the soldiers came into

---

[18]Jerome, *Letter* 127.12, trans. W. H. Fremantle, G. Lewis and W. G. Martley, in *NPNF*, 2nd series, vol. 6, ed. Philip Schaff and Henry Wace (Buffalo, N.Y.: Christian Literature Publishing, 1893), revised and edited for New Advent by Kevin Knight, http://www.newadvent.org/fathers/3001127.htm.

[19]Virgil, *Virgil's Aeneid*, trans. John Dryden (New York: P. F. Collier, 1909), p. 115.

the house of Marcella, a saintly Roman aristocrat who had
renounced her wealth for an ascetic Christian life—but who
unfortunately still lived in a rich-looking house. Since he
had heard that Principia was an eyewitness, we can imagine
that Jerome was unusually careful with his facts.

> Meantime, as was natural in a scene of such confusion,
> one of the bloodstained victors found his way into Mar-
> cella's house. Now it is my job to say what I have heard,
> to relate what holy men have seen; for there were some
> such present and they say that you too were with her in
> the hour of danger. When the soldiers entered, they say,
> she received them without any look of alarm; and when
> they asked her for gold she pointed to her coarse dress
> to show them that she had no buried treasure. However,
> they would not believe in her self-chosen poverty, but
> scourged her and beat her with cudgels. They say she felt
> no pain, but she threw herself at their feet and pleaded
> with tears for you, that you might not be taken from her,
> or owing to your youth have to endure what she as an
> old woman had no occasion to fear. Christ softened their
> hard hearts, and even among bloodstained swords natu-
> ral affection asserted its rights. The barbarians conveyed
> both you and her to the basilica of the apostle Paul, that
> you might find there either a place of safety or, if not
> that, at least a tomb.[20]

Marcella never recovered from that night; she died a few
days later, probably from her injuries.

It was not the end for Rome, but it felt like the end of
the world. It had been eight hundred years since a foreign
enemy had entered the city. The impregnable capital of
the world was at the mercy of the barbarians.

[20] Jerome, *Letter* 127.12–13.

Nevertheless, Rome continued and even recovered. But now the people in the city had to worry about barbarian raids. And they were beginning to learn that emperors couldn't or wouldn't save them. They would have to look for help to the only effective leader they had: the pope.

They learned that lesson well when the fearsome Attila the Hun came roaring through the empire, bearing down on the city of Rome. Attila and his horde were an apocalypse on horseback. No Roman force could stand in their way. But Pope Leo went out from Rome, unarmed, and talked to Attila. No one knows what he said, but Attila turned around and went away, and Rome was spared. It would be hard to put the thing more clearly than that. Emperors and armies are worthless; only the bishop of Rome can save his city.

Yet even Leo the Great, as history remembers him, could not save Rome from the Vandals in 455. The best he could do was work out an agreement that the inhabitants wouldn't be massacred while the Vandals pillaged the city for ten days. They were so thorough about it that they gave their name to the act of wanton destruction, which we still call *vandal*ism today.

As provinces fell away, the Roman Empire in the West was reduced to Italy and a few surrounding areas, but there was a Western emperor until 476, when the last one sent his imperial insignia off to Constantinople, saying there was no longer a need for two emperors. What he meant was that a barbarian general named Odoacer had decided to make himself king of Italy rather than just the power behind the throne. Theoretically, Odoacer was under the authority of the emperor of Constantinople, but for all practical purposes, the Roman Empire was finished in the West. Not completely finished: the Eastern emperor did manage to have Odoacer kicked out after a few years, but

only by sending another Goth—the much more capable
Theodoric—to get the job done. Then Theodoric became
king of Italy.

After Theodoric died, the emperor Justinian—we'll
hear more about him later—decided to retake Italy from
the Goths. His generals succeeded for a while, but Italy
was devastated by the years of war. At the low point of the
Gothic Wars, the city of Rome was completely depop-
ulated; the Gothic general who sacked it in 546 found
five hundred people within the walls. The Dark Ages
had begun.

Gregory the Great

Because the complex organization of Roman government
had fallen apart, the popes had to take up more and more
authority. In 590, when Rome was still suffering from
waves of barbarians—this time the Lombards—a pope
named Gregory came to the throne of Peter and began to
reimagine the Church as a spiritual empire.

By any standard, Gregory the Great was an extraordinary leader. He reformed the liturgy: we still call the characteristic music of Catholic worship Gregorian chant. He
wrote a book of dialogues of the saints that was so influential that he is still remembered in the Eastern churches
as Saint Gregory the Dialogist. In the English-speaking
world, he's remembered as the pope who organized a mission to the pagan English, which began the conversion of
England to Christianity. Closer to home, he organized the
Roman Church into an effective government for the city,
keeping careful accounts of the alms given to the Church
and organizing the distribution to make sure they went
where they were needed.

Gregory the Great marks the division between the ancient world and the Middle Ages. He saw the problem of his time clearly: no one else was taking care of basic needs, so the Church would have to step in and do some organizing. And Gregory was a genius at organizing.

It was Gregory who built the papacy into the closest thing the West would have to a real government for the next few centuries. Once again, all roads would lead to Rome. Once again, Rome would be the capital of the known world. But it would be a different kind of dominion.

4

Alexandria

All we can see as we sail toward the coast is water, except for a white pillar on the horizon, growing larger and larger, until it resolves itself into a huge skyscraper, glinting in the Mediterranean sun.

The experienced travelers on board pay no attention to it, but all the tourists and first-timers point and gossip. This is the famous lighthouse of Alexandria, the Pharos, one of the Seven Wonders of the World, and it's worth coming to Alexandria just to sail past it and get dizzy looking up at it.

Alexandria is full of wonders. The city comes into view now, gleaming white, almost as if the buildings were lit from within. Temples and palaces are arranged with an eye for the picturesque and impressive. The cityscape looks like a fresco of an ideal city in some aristocrat's palace.

As soon as we land, we realize that the whole world comes to Alexandria. The sailors and merchants and stevedores are shouting in a dozen different languages as they load and unload exotic treasures from around the world. The broad streets are full of tourists like us from far-off lands—India, Persia, Ethiopia—all pointing out the sights.

Suddenly we turn a corner, and there's a big crowd listening to some noisy orator and shouting their approval. The orator sounds angry. He's yelling something that sounds like a slogan—"There was a time when he was not!" The crowd roars. They like that slogan.

We turn around and leave that square quickly. Our friends who know the city warned us to stay away from mobs like that in Alexandria. You never know what might happen, they said.

Founding a Showplace

The story of Alexandria, like the story of Antioch, begins with Alexander, the Macedonian boy who conquered the world.

The Macedonians seemed to have a thing about proving they were just as good as the other Greeks, probably because the other Greeks persisted in regarding them as hicks with no intellectual life. Athenians thought of Macedonia the way New Yorkers think of Wichita. Alexander's father, Philip, had brought in Aristotle, the most famous philosopher in Athens, to be his son's tutor, hoping to take the hick edge off him and give him some big-city polish.

In a way, it worked. Alexander kept all his father's genius for effective violence, but wherever he went, he brought a conviction that Greek culture was superior. He spread that culture from Macedonia to India, founding towns called Alexandria wherever he went.

The one that really took off was Alexandria in Egypt. It was designed as a rational city, the sort of city a philosopher would draw in the sand if you said, "Make me a map of the ideal city." Its streets were laid out in a grid, like Washington or Orlando, rather than the haphazard accumulation of centuries of tracks that made up most Greek cities. And whereas the streets in most ancient cities were narrow lanes where people pushed past one another on foot, these were broad boulevards where you could ride a horse or drive a chariot. The architect was Dinocrates of Rhodes, and he designed a city that Alexander would have been proud of had he lived to see it.[1]

By a tremendous feat of engineering, Alexander's builders managed to make a safe port on the notoriously unsafe Egyptian seacoast. They connected it to the Nile by canals, and Egypt had a new great city—a thoroughly Greek city that linked it to the rest of the Mediterranean world.

The big problem for sailors approaching Alexandria was landing. First of all, the seacoast was monotonously regular, and the city was practically invisible until you were right there. Second, the water near the city was full of shoals and reefs that made it dangerous to deviate from the main channel. The Pharos, or lighthouse, was the solution to that problem. It stood on the offshore island of Pharos, which gave its name to the building. It was as tall as a thirty-story skyscraper, so it was visible on the horizon from many miles out. In bad weather or at night, the beacon at the top shone out and guided sailors safely into Alexandria's capacious port.

Yes, Alexander would have been very proud of his city. But he died at the age of thirty-two, having conquered his way to India but making it only as far back as Babylon before he expired.

The Cultural Capital of the World

As we remember from the case of Antioch, Alexander's world empire split into multiple empires headed by his

---

[1] Peter A. Clayton and Martin Price, *The Seven Wonders of the Ancient World* (New York: Barnes & Noble, 1993), p. 139.

most successful generals. The one who got Egypt was named Ptolemy. He led a long line of Ptolemys and Cleopatras that finally ended when the last of the line pressed an asp to Cleopatra's bosom.

Ptolemy had a thing for culture. He wanted to make his capital the most renowned city on earth, and perhaps because he was a Macedonian, he thought in terms of learning and culture when he envisioned making a magnificent city.

Because they were rich, the Ptolemys succeeded in making Alexandria the center of learning in the world. Athens could still boast of its Academy and its famous philosophers, but the best of them moved to Alexandria to be where the money was and where the books were.

The Alexandrian Museum was a place where scholars were lured by the delightful promises of free room and board and *no taxes*.[2] It was a good life for a philosopher to sit and eat good food and talk with other great minds, and they came to Alexandria in droves.

The Library of Alexandria was the Ptolemys' proudest achievement. It was meant to have a copy of every book in the world—or, even better, to have the original manuscript. If ships that came into port were carrying books, the customs officials would borrow the books to be copied for the library. Then the copy would be returned to the original owner, and the original would stay in the library. (This famous library was destroyed a number of times, but its remnants probably lingered on until past the Arab conquest.)

With opportunities for trade that no other city could match and an exciting intellectual atmosphere, Alexandria rapidly grew to be the world's biggest city, until it

[2] Ibid., p. 142.

was passed up by Rome. Though it was the capital of
Egypt, it was a majority-Greek city. But it had a very large
and significant Jewish population too. They were mostly
Greek-speaking Jews, and they made Alexandria the most
important Jewish city outside Jerusalem.

Because the great library needed a copy of every book
in the world, it needed a copy of the Jewish Scriptures.
And, of course, it needed a Greek copy so that the current Ptolemy, Ptolemy Philadelphus, and the other philosophers who used the library could understand the
books. So Ptolemy rounded up seventy of the greatest
Jewish scholars in Alexandria and set them to translating the Hebrew Scriptures into Greek. The translation
they came up with is still called the Septuagint, from the
Greek word for "seventy".

That is the traditional origin story of the Septuagint, the
standard Greek version of the Old Testament. It may be a
legend, but like all old legends, it tells us a lot about the
people who believed it, even if it isn't true. Succeeding
generations added miraculous details to the legend. They
said that, instead of the seventy scholars dividing up the
work, Ptolemy separated them and had each one individ-
ually translate all the Scriptures; when he compared their
work, the translations were identical. This proved that
the translators were divinely inspired. It sounds unlikely
to us, but more than one of the Church Fathers accepted
that story. Not the skeptical and scientific-minded Saint
Jerome, though. He had translated Scripture himself and
thought the story was a ridiculous legend.

The Septuagint became the standard Greek translation
of the Scriptures for all Greek-speaking Jews. The New
Testament writers all wrote in Greek (with the possible
exception of Matthew—a minority of scholars accept the
tradition that he wrote his Gospel in Hebrew first), and

when they wanted to quote the Old Testament, they usually quoted the Septuagint version.

Philo of Alexandria

The Jewish community grew and prospered and became a big part of Alexandria's civic life. According to one Jewish writer, two out of five districts in the city were inhabited by Jews. That Jewish writer was Philo of Alexandria, also known as Philo Judaeus—the greatest Jewish thinker to come out of Alexandria. Philo lived at the time of Christ—he was born before Jesus and lived on after the Ascension. There's no evidence that he was Christian or even heard the Gospel, but some of his ideas would be so influential in the Christian thought of Alexandria that he almost counts as an honorary Church Father.

Philo was an important man in the Jewish community, which meant he was an important man in Alexandria. During the reign of Caligula, one of Rome's periodic mad emperors, riots broke out in Alexandria. Philo says they were provoked by the pagan mob. "I do not mean the ordinary and well-regulated population of the city," he says, "but the mob which, out of its restlessness and love of an unquiet and disorderly life, was always filling every place with tumult and confusion, and who, because of their habitual idleness and laziness, were full of treachery and revolutionary plans."[3] We'll meet that restless and disorderly mob again and again in the history of Alexandria. Of all the ancient cities, Alexandria was the most prone

[3] Philo of Alexandria, *Flaccus* 6, in *The Works of Philo Judaeus*, trans. C.D. Yonge (London: Henry G. Bohn, 1855). Subsequent citations of works by Philo are from this translation.

to riots. This time the pagan mob decided they wanted to show those Jews by putting up pagan statues in the synagogues. Flaccus, the Roman governor, encouraged them. Predictable riots followed, in which many Jews were murdered and much of their property was destroyed. Like Hitler after Kristallnacht, Flaccus punished the Jews for the violence against them.

Philo was chosen as one of the representatives of the Jewish community to take a petition to the emperor. He left us a firsthand account of Caligula's court, showing us a mad emperor with the attention span of a mayfly. The account is comical to us two millennia later, but it wasn't funny to Philo and his companions, who were wondering the whole time whether they would suddenly be executed on a whim of the childish Caligula. The fact that Philo was chosen for this mission, though, shows us that he was influential in the community, and his ideas must have been influential as well.

Those ideas are what we remember him for today. Philo was one of the most important interpreters of Scripture in history. He was one of the founders of the allegorical method of interpretation, which looks for deeper meanings behind the literal meaning of the biblical accounts.

He explains his method briefly when he is dealing with the history of Joseph: "It is worth while, however, after having thus explained the literal account given to us of these events, to proceed to explain also the figurative meaning concealed under that account. For we say that nearly all, or at least the greater part, of the history of the giving of the law is full of allegories."[4]

Now, Philo does not mean that the history of Joseph and the other stories in the Bible never really happened. What he means is that the events, and the way they are

[4] Philo, *On Joseph* 6.

told, can lead us to think about symbolic meanings inherent in the narrative. For example, Joseph had a coat of many colors, and he was sold as a slave, and his brothers let their father believe he had been torn by wild beasts. When Joseph became a political leader in Egypt, all these things had appropriate symbolic meanings.

> It is not without a particular and correct meaning that Joseph is said to have had a coat of many colors.... I conceive that the man immersed in political affairs is of necessity a multiform man, assuming many different appearances, one in time of peace and another in time of war; and a different character according as those who are opposed to him are numerous or few in number, withstanding a small number with vigorous resolution, but using persuasion and gentle means towards a large body....
>
> It was appropriately said that the man was sold. For the haranguer of the people and the demagogue, mounting the tribunal, like slaves who are being sold and exposed to view, is a slave instead of a free man, by reason of the honors which he seems to be receiving, being led away by ten thousand masters.
>
> The same person is also represented as having been torn by wild beasts; and vainglory, which lies in wait for a man, is an untamable wild beast, tearing and destroying all who give in to it.[5]

This allegorical method was not unique to Philo. Saint Paul, a contemporary of Philo, also saw allegories in the Old Testament stories. In fact, Paul may have invented the word "allegory" in his famous analysis of the history of Sarah and Hagar (see Gal 4:24). But Philo used the method constantly. It was his thing.

[5] Ibid., 7.

For Christians, one of the most striking aspects of Philo's thought is his idea that God created the world through "his first-born Word".[6] This Word is the eternal image of God. "For even if we are not yet suitable to be called the sons of God, still we may deserve to be called the children of his eternal image, of his most sacred Word; for the image of God is his most ancient Word."[7] This is not quite orthodox Christianity, but it's so close to what Christians believe about Jesus that it's no wonder Christians preserved so many of the manuscripts of Philo's work.

Philo was well educated in Greek philosophy, and he believed that Plato and Moses were on the same track. Moses was divinely inspired, of course, but Plato's work also helped us understand the nature of God and creation.

These ideas must have been circulating in the Jewish community in Alexandria. Just as we would expect, when Christianity in Alexandria started to develop its own distinctive style of thought, two of its distinctive features were familiarity with Greek philosophy and an allegorical approach to Scripture.

Clement of Alexandria

Tradition says that Saint Mark, the disciple of Peter who wrote the second Gospel, brought Christianity to Alexandria. With such a large Jewish community already influenced by Philo's ideas of the Word, Christianity took root quickly in the city, and soon Alexandria became one of the most important centers of Christian thought. "A school of sacred learning, which continues to our day, was

[6] Philo, *On the Confusion of Tongues* 28.
[7] Ibid.

established there in ancient times," the ancient historian Eusebius tells us, "and as we have been informed was managed by men of great ability and zeal for divine things."[8] We don't know exactly what was meant by a "school". But whether it was a formal organization or a looser tradition of Christian learning, the school of Alexandria was rivaled only by the school of Antioch as a center of Christian thought.

The first important teacher in Alexandria whose name we know was Saint Pantaenus, who died in about 200. He was a Stoic philosopher who became a Christian, and he brought all his knowledge of Greek philosophy with him. As one of the chief Christian teachers of Alexandria, he had a deep influence on the teachers who followed him—especially his disciple Clement, known as Saint Clement of Alexandria to distinguish him from Saint Clement of Rome.

From his teacher, Clement learned the importance of every kind of learning for the Christian who was called to explain the faith. Clement had a very good traditional Greek education, and he could quote all the important philosophers at length.

But why would a Christian study pagan philosophy? Clement answered "that Scripture calls every secular science or art by the one name 'wisdom' ... and that artistic and skillful invention is from God".[9] Wherever we find useful knowledge, God is responsible for it, even if the

[8] Eusebius, *Church History* 5.10, trans. Arthur Cushman McGiffert, in *NPNF*, 2nd series, vol. 1, ed. Philip Schaff and Henry Wace (Buffalo, N.Y.: Christian Literature Publishing, 1890), revised and edited for New Advent by Kevin Knight, http://www.newadvent.org/fathers/250105.htm.

[9] Clement of Alexandria, *The Stromata* 1.4, trans. William Wilson, in *ANF*, vol. 2, ed. Alexander Roberts, James Donaldson, and A. Cleveland Coxe (Buffalo, N.Y.: Christian Literature Publishing, 1885), revised and edited for New Advent by Kevin Knight, https://www.newadvent.org/fathers/02101.htm.

people who possess it do not know and worship God. The Greeks became very good at reasoning and logic, and that was God's plan for them.

> Before the advent of the Lord, philosophy was necessary to the Greeks for righteousness. And now it becomes conducive to piety: it is a kind of preparatory training to those who reach faith through demonstration. For "your foot," it is said, "will not stumble" (Proverbs 3:23), if you attribute what is good, whether belonging to the Greeks or to us, to Providence. For God is the cause of all good things. But he is the cause of some primarily, such as the Old and the New Testament, and of others by consequence, as philosophy. Perhaps, too, philosophy was given to the Greeks directly and primarily, till the Lord should call the Greeks. For philosophy was a custodian to bring the Greek mind to Christ, as the Law was the custodian of the Hebrews (see Galatians 3:25). Philosophy, therefore, was a preparation, paving the way for him who is perfected in Christ.[10]

There was nothing new in applying Greek learning to Christian thought. Saint Paul himself quoted Greek authors when he thought he would reach his listeners better that way (see, for example, Acts 17:28). But Clement explicitly insisted that Greek learning was useful and even important to a Christian. In Clement's eyes, it was a mistake to try to understand Christian faith without having a good classical education. Of course there were good uneducated Christians, but someone who undertakes to explain the faith needs all the tools education can provide.

> Some, who think themselves naturally gifted, do not wish to touch either philosophy or logic. They do not even wish to learn natural science. They demand bare faith

[10] Ibid., 1.5.

alone, as if they wished to gather fruit from the vine right away, without putting any work into it. Now the Lord is figuratively described as the vine, from which, with care and the art of cultivation, according to the word, the fruit is to be gathered. We must lop, dig, bind, and do the rest of the work. The pruning knife, I should think, and the pickax, and the other agricultural implements, are necessary for the culture of the vine, so that it may produce edible fruit. And as in farming, so also in medicine: the one who has learned effectively is the one who has practiced the various lessons, so as to be able to cultivate and to heal. So also here, I call someone truly learned who brings everything to bear on the truth; so that, taking out what is useful from geometry, and music, and grammar, and philosophy itself, he guards the faith against assault.[11]

Clement left Alexandria when the persecution of Christians flared up under the emperor Severus. That same persecution nearly killed the next famous Christian intellectual in Alexandria—but not quite, because the would-be martyr's mom was too quick for him.

Origen

Origen was born into a Christian family in the year 185. His family was well off, and Origen got an excellent classical education. But then came that persecution.

It started, as it usually did, when the latest emperor, Septimius Severus, decided things would have to shape up and people would have to toe the line. This persecution was an especially bad one, and Origen's father, Leonidas, was arrested and held for execution. Though Origen was still only a teenager, he desperately wanted to follow his

[11] Ibid., 1.9.

father to martyrdom. As Eusebius tells us, he was saved only because his mother was not only loving but also a little devious: "Truly the end of his life would have been very near had not the divine and heavenly Providence, for the benefit of many, prevented his desire through the agency of his mother. For, at first, entreating him, she begged him to have compassion on her motherly feelings toward him; but finding that, when he had learned that his father had been seized and imprisoned, he was set the more resolutely, and completely carried away with his zeal for martyrdom, she hid all his clothing, and thus compelled him to remain at home."[12] Sometimes a mother just has to be sneaky.

Now Origen had to support his mother and himself. He went to work as a teacher, but he didn't keep that job for long. He was needed elsewhere.

The persecution had killed or exiled most of the competent Christian teachers in Alexandria. But, like all the persecutions, it was producing thousands of converts, and they needed to be catechized. Young Origen had a keen mind and an exceptional education, and when the bishop asked him to take over the catechetical program, he said yes right away.

It soon became obvious to everyone who met him that this young man had an exceptional mind. It was so obvious that a wealthy donor, converted to Christianity by Origen's persuasion, provided him with a staff of secretaries to take down his dictation. With that help, Origen became the most prolific writer in all antiquity, and perhaps one of the most prolific of all time. Saint Jerome gives a *short* list of his works that numbers eight hundred, but he says that another (now-lost) list numbered more than two thousand.

---

[12] Eusebius, *Church History* 6.2.4–5, http://www.newadvent.org/fathers/250 106.htm.

With his Greek philosophical training, Origen tried to put Christian learning on a systematic basis. He also founded Christian biblical text criticism by putting together the Hexapla, an arrangement of the Bible with parallel columns of the Hebrew text, a transliteration of the Hebrew into Greek letters, and four different Greek translations.

You may have noticed that Origen doesn't have "Saint" in front of his name. His interpretations of Scripture were sometimes very speculative, and he veered into territory that would be heretical today. It wasn't heresy then, because the Church had not yet made definitive pronouncements, and Origen was always willing to submit his ideas to the authority of the Church. Most theologians today would say that Origen was not a heretic, but he was sometimes wrong. Not all theological mistakes amount to heresy.

In his late sixties, Origen finally got his wish to suffer for Christ. In the persecution under Decius, he was imprisoned and tortured, with orders to keep him alive as long as possible. He lived to the end of the persecution, but he died shortly afterward from the effects of the mistreatment.

The persecutions finally ended, as we remember, when Constantine legalized Christianity in 313. The last of the bishops of Alexandria to be martyred was Peter. Achillas, his chosen successor, died of natural causes after only six months. Alexander became the first bishop to lead the Church in Alexandria in the post-persecution age.

Arius versus Athanasius

Alexander was a good bishop, a competent administrator who taught the Gospel the way it had always been taught. But in a city like Alexandria, he would naturally have to deal with troublemakers. It was only a matter of time before some clever priest thought he was smarter than his bishop. When it did happen, the trouble came from one who was already a known troublemaker.

Arius was a priest who had been trained in Antioch, and perhaps he absorbed too much of the well-known literal approach to interpreting Scripture that the theologians of Antioch taught. He had been excommunicated once already for siding with a schismatic who was against readmitting Christians who had lapsed during the persecutions and later repented. But Alexander's predecessor had taken Arius back into communion, and Arius was building up a reputation in some circles as a clever logician. When Achillas died after only six months, Arius couldn't see any reason why he himself shouldn't be bishop of Alexandria. The majority of the Alexandrian Church disagreed and chose Alexander instead.

So when Alexander tried to explain the Trinity, Arius thought he knew better, as the ancient historian Socrates Scholasticus tells us. One day, fearlessly exercising his functions for the instruction and government of the Church, Alexander tried,

> in the presence of the presbytery and the rest of his clergy, to explain, with perhaps too philosophical minuteness, that great theological mystery, the Unity of the Holy Trinity. A certain one of the presbyters under his jurisdiction, whose name was Arius, possessed no inconsiderable skill in logic. Imagining that the bishop was subtly teaching the same view of this subject as Sabellius the Libyan, [he] from love of controversy took the opposite opinion to that of the Libyan, and (as he thought) vigorously responded to what was said by the bishop. "If the Father begot the Son," he said, "he that was begotten had a beginning of existence: and from this it is evident that there was a time when the

Son was not. It therefore necessarily follows that he had his substance from nothing."[13]

Accusing your bishop of heresy is usually not the way to get ahead in the Church. But Alexandria loved a controversy, all the more because Arius and his party were good at coming up with slogans that a mob could chant. "There was a time when he was not" in Greek has a nursery-rhyme lilt to it that was easy to remember. Nobody knew it at the time, but this little confrontation was setting up the dispute that would rip through the Church for two centuries and bring the emperor himself into ecclesiastical affairs. Alexander excommunicated Arius again, but Arius had powerful supporters—especially among people who would like to see the bishop of Alexandria put in his place. And of course there was that unquiet and disorderly mob who were always looking for any excuse to start a riot. A lot of them were nominally Christian, but they still loved a good fight.

It was a fight that spread all over the eastern half of the Roman Empire. Eventually, the emperor Constantine himself got into it: he decided to settle it by calling all the bishops together in a big meeting, which we remember as the Council of Nicaea in 325.

It was true that the bishop of Alexandria was a very important figure, and even the bishop of Rome was against Arius. But Arius had the support of some highly placed figures in the Church and was confident in his ability to outargue Alexander. What he didn't count on was that Alexander had a brilliant young man with him, a fellow

[13] Socrates Scholasticus, *Ecclesiastical History* 1.5, trans. A.C. Zenos, in *NPNF*, 2nd series, vol. 2, ed. Philip Schaff and Henry Wace (Buffalo: Christian Literature Publishing, 1890), revised and edited for New Advent by Kevin Knight, http://www.newadvent.org/fathers/26011.htm.

called Athanasius whose small frame held a giant intellect. Arius was polished and polite, but Athanasius was the better in argument. The council decided in favor of what Alexander had been teaching, and what the Church had been teaching all along: that the Son was coeternal with the Father. Arius was out.

It should have been all over, but it wasn't. Arius had a shrewd and devious supporter in Eusebius of Nicomedia, bishop of the city where the emperor had made his residence. (Eusebius was a very common name; this is a different Eusebius from the historian who lived at the same time.) For Eusebius, Arius was the means to put the powerful bishop of Alexandria in his place and boost his own power in the process. And since Alexander, who was old and feeble, died not long after the Council of Nicaea, Athanasius had become the bishop of Alexandria.

No bishop ever had a rougher time than Athanasius. The Arians gained the support of the emperors who followed Constantine, and then Julian the Apostate came with his evenhanded contempt for all Christians. Officially, Athanasius was exiled five times, not counting the various times he had to run for his life unofficially.

But Athanasius had the support of the large group of Christians who held to the original faith in Alexandria. You could tell where the crowd's sympathies really lay, because every time Athanasius came back, they greeted him with an impromptu parade.

Meanwhile, in spite of all the dangers he had to face, Athanasius kept writing and writing. In his treatises against the Arians, he clarified and developed orthodox Catholic theology, so that "Athanasian" became the term for the traditional Trinitarian theology that Athanasius fought for.

After a long and productive life of trouble, Athanasius lived to see an orthodox emperor and a momentary triumph for Athanasian Christianity. He died in his own

bed, surrounded by his clergy and mourned by hundreds
of thousands of his flock in the city.

But of course the troubles weren't over. Alexandria's
troubles were never over.

Cyril

"The Alexandrians are more delighted with a riot than any
other people; and if they can find a pretext, they will break
out into the most intolerable excesses. Then it is scarcely
possible to check their impetuosity until there has been
much bloodshed."[14] So wrote the historian Socrates Scholasticus, making the same observation that Philo of Alexandria had made a long time before. Much of the history
of Alexandria is a history of riots and their consequences.

In the year 412, Theophilus, then bishop of Alexandria, died, and there was a big fight over who should be
his successor. Significantly, the Roman commander took
one side, but the mob took another, and the mob won.
Theophilus' nephew Cyril became bishop, "with more
power", says the historian Socrates, "than his uncle ever
had. For from that time on the bishops of Alexandria,
going beyond the limits of their sacerdotal functions, took
up the administration of secular matters."[15]

Cyril showed that power when he expelled the Jews
from Alexandria. We don't know exactly what this "expul-
sion" was or how many of the Jews it involved. But it does
show how much power the bishop had.

The Jews were still a significant part of the population,
and a certain group of Jewish troublemakers, every bit
as troublesome as the Christian and pagan troublemakers,

---

[14] Ibid., 7.13, http://www.newadvent.org/fathers/26017.htm.
[15] Ibid., 7.7.

had hatched a plot to massacre a bunch of random Christians at night. Even though the Jews seem to have had the protection of the governor, Cyril was able to order them, or at least the troublesome elements, to leave the city, and he had the mob to back him up.

Not long afterward came the most notorious incident of mob violence in Alexandria: the murder of the philosopher Hypatia. Hypatia was unique in pagan culture. Christian women had been making important contributions to the faith for a long time: we remember Marcella in Rome, who was the center of an intellectual circle of Christian thinkers who relied on her advice. But when you search classical history for pagan women philosophers, Hypatia is almost the only name that comes up. She was well regarded by both pagan and Christian intellectuals, and a number of soon-to-be famous Christians were her students. But the mob hated her.

There were a lot of reasons for the troublemakers in Alexandria to hate Hypatia. She was pagan when the mob had become nominally Christian. She was a woman, and what business did a woman have being smart in public?

But the thing that stirred the mob to violence was a rumor that Hypatia was souring the Roman governor's relationship with the bishop. By this time, the bishop of Alexandria was so powerful that it would be hard to say who was more important in governing the city. Cyril was popular with the mob, and if the governor was against Cyril, it was a bad time to be governor.

As Hypatia was riding home in her carriage, the mob fell on her, pulled her out of the carriage, and dragged her into a church, where they hacked her to pieces with whatever sharp objects they could find. Then they took the mangled corpse outside city limits and set it on fire.

Some people blame Cyril for the mob that slaughtered her. Some anti-Christian writers blame Christianity in general. But no one could control the Alexandrian mob, as Philo and Socrates both told us. At any rate, we should remember that the only reason we know about the incident at all is because Christian historians wrote it down and deplored it as a disgraceful example of mob violence. "An act so inhuman could not fail to bring the greatest disgrace, not only on Cyril, but also on the whole Alexandrian church", wrote Socrates. "And surely nothing can be further from the spirit of Christianity than allowing massacres, fights, and that sort of thing."[16] The people who get angriest at Christians in general are parroting the rhetoric of the Christian historian who told them the story.

Cyril versus Nestorius

The next big dispute in Eastern Christianity was a swing of the pendulum in the opposite direction from Arius. In 328, a scholarly gentleman named Nestorius was appointed bishop of Constantinople. He was the kind of pedantic thinker who loved to make technical distinctions, and when he said in a homily that Mary wasn't *technically* the Mother of God, the Church blew up around him. We'll hear the whole tragic tale of Nestorius when we visit Ephesus. But we can't leave Alexandria without mentioning the leading part Cyril of Alexandria played in fighting the Nestorian heresy.

When the news reached Alexandria, Cyril immediately took up the fight against Nestorius, supported at a distance by the pope in Rome. Nestorius, thinking he was obviously in the right, persuaded the emperor to call a council to settle the dispute—but he was dismayed when he discovered that the council would be held in Ephesus,

[16] Ibid., 7.15.

a center of the cult of Mary, and that the president would be the bishop of Alexandria.

Nestorius was counting on support from his old friends in Syria, but they were delayed. Cyril, following the rules to the letter, convened the council on time, and Socrates tells us how Cyril goaded Nestorius into making such a shocking statement that the other bishops all had to back away from him. Cyril began a sharp skirmish of words designed to terrify Nestorius, whom he strongly disliked. When many had declared that Christ was God, Nestorius said, "I cannot term him God who was two and three months old. I am therefore clear of your blood, and shall in future come no more among you."[17] After that, Nestorius walked out. The other bishops who stayed shook their heads and murmured. That man had just said that the child Jesus *wasn't God.*

The council condemned Nestorius. But then his friends from Syria arrived, and they formed a counter-council and condemned Cyril.

Nestorius was deposed and spent his last years in exile. But some of his Eastern followers never deserted him. He is still counted as a saint in some Eastern churches. But in the Catholic Church, Cyril and Alexandria had triumphed.

Alexandria has a long history after that, but Cyril was probably the peak of its influence in the Church. In the 600s, when Arab armies poured through the East, Alexandria held out only a little longer than the rest of Egypt. As in most of the Eastern cities, the Arab conquerors ruled a mostly Christian population for centuries after they took over. Even today, about one in ten Egyptians is a Christian, and Alexandria is still the seat of a pope, which is an honorary title of the Coptic patriarch.

[17] Ibid., 7.34.

5

Ephesus

Ephesus bursts into Christian history as the scene of a riot by the souvenir salesmen.

We've already visited Jerusalem, Antioch, Rome, and Alexandria, and each of those is a living city. Jerusalem is still thriving and fought over today; Antioch has become a small but substantial city in Turkey; Rome is still a major capital filled with evidence of its centuries of history; Alexandria is a bustling metropolis on the Mediterranean.

But Ephesus is just gone.

You can visit the site today. Archaeologists have dug up some impressive ruins. They've put them together in picturesque arrangements for tourists to take selfies in front of. But it's an uninhabited wasteland. When the last tour bus leaves in the evening, no one is left but the birds and the lizards.

That makes it harder to envision how important Ephesus was, both to the Roman world and to Christian history.

But when we remember the riot of the silversmiths, we can begin to tease out some of that lost importance.

The Wonderful Temple of Artemis

When we visited Alexandria, we passed one of the Seven Wonders of the ancient world: the lighthouse at Alexandria.

Ephesus was home to another one of the famous wonders: the Temple of Artemis, or Diana to the Romans.

It probably looked like other Greek temples but on a scale we find hard to imagine. It was as long as a football field and a half. It had more than a hundred columns. It was as tall as a six-story building—not nearly as tall as the Pharos, but still tall enough to seem dizzyingly high. An ancient Greek poet named Antipater thought it was the most wonderful of all the Seven Wonders:

> I have set eyes on the wall of lofty Babylon on which is a road for chariots, and the statue of Zeus by the Alpheus, and the hanging gardens, and the colossus of the Sun, and the huge labor of the high pyramids, and the vast tomb of Mausolus; but when I saw the house of Artemis that mounted to the clouds, those other marvels lost their brilliancy, and I said, "Lo, apart from Olympus, the Sun never looked on anything so grand."[1]

That poem, by the way, is the earliest known list of the Seven Wonders of the World, although it's clear the poet expects us to know what he's talking about, so it must have been a well-known list already. You may also have noticed the slight variation: the Pharos isn't there. Instead, Antipater mentions the walls of Babylon.

Pilgrims from all over the Roman world came to see the temple. And wherever tourists are, people are ready to sell them souvenirs. The silversmiths of Ephesus did a brisk business in little silver replicas of the temple and statue. It was an expensive souvenir, certainly, but it was a thing you could take home with you and put on your hearth to show you had made the trip to Ephesus and to remind you of the magnificent things you had seen there.

[1] W.R. Paton, trans., *The Greek Anthology* 9.58 (London: William Heinemann, 1916).

Then came Paul preaching that idols like Diana of the Ephesians were false gods, nothing but stone and metal and wood. And he was winning converts. He even had friends among the ruling class.

What would happen to that flourishing souvenir business if these Christians succeeded—unlikely as it seems—in persuading people that Artemis was not really a divine being? Who would buy the little silver replicas then?

This is the story Luke tells in the nineteenth chapter of the Acts of the Apostles:

> About that time there arose no little stir concerning the Way. For a man named Demetrius, a silversmith, who made silver shrines of Artemis, brought no little business to the craftsmen. These he gathered together, with the workmen of like occupation, and said, "Men, you know that from this business we have our wealth. And you see and hear that not only at Ephesus but almost throughout all Asia this Paul has persuaded and turned away a considerable company of people, saying that gods made with hands are not gods. And there is danger not only that this trade of ours may come into disrepute but also that the temple of the great goddess Artemis may count for nothing, and that she may even be deposed from her magnificence, she whom all Asia and the world worship."
>
> When they heard this they were enraged, and cried out, "Great is Artemis of the Ephesians!" (19:23–28)

What follows is one of the most vivid descriptions of a riot to come down from the ancient world. We know that cities were full of riots, but Luke, with his physician's eye for detail, gives us the anatomy of a riot. This is what he says: "So the city was filled with the confusion; and they rushed together into the theater, dragging with them Gaius and Aristarchus, Macedonians who were Paul's companions in travel. Paul wished to go in among the crowd, but the disciples would not let him; some of the Asiarchs also, who were friends of his, sent to him and begged him not to venture into the theater" (19:29–31).

To interrupt Luke for a moment: we don't know exactly what position Asiarchs held, but we know they were important officials in the administration of the province. This may tell us something about why the silversmiths were so agitated: Paul was making friends in high places. We also notice that the rioters assembled in the theater. This is what we hear over and over again: when a riot begins, it usually starts at the theater or the stadium, the places where people were used to assembling in big crowds and where speeches could be heard by an excited mob. In Ephesus, the theater was huge; modern historians think it was the largest in the Roman Empire. That may give us some idea of the size of the mob.

Luke continues, giving us a remarkable portrait of mob psychology: "Some cried one thing, some another; for the assembly was in confusion, and most of them did not know why they had come together. Some of the crowd prompted Alexander, whom the Jews had put forward. And Alexander motioned with his hand, wishing to make a defense to the people. But when they recognized that he was a Jew, for about two hours they all with one voice cried out, 'Great is Artemis of the Ephesians!'" (19:32–34).

This was a bad and dangerous situation. A mob chanting slogans can turn violent quickly. It looked as though they might turn violent against Jews in the city, and there were a lot of Jews in Ephesus. The city authorities were alarmed, and one of them managed to get up in front of the mob and get their attention, as Luke tells us:

> And when the town clerk had quieted the crowd, he said, "Men of Ephesus, what man is there who does not know that the city of the Ephesians is temple keeper of the great

Artemis, and of the sacred stone that fell from the sky? Seeing then that these things cannot be contradicted, you ought
to be quiet and do nothing rash. For you have brought these
men here who are neither sacrilegious nor blasphemers of
our goddess. If therefore Demetrius and the craftsmen with
him have a complaint against any one, the courts are open,
and there are proconsuls; let them bring charges against one
another. But if you seek anything further, it shall be settled in the regular assembly. For we are in danger of being
charged with rioting today, there being no cause that we
can give to justify this commotion." (19:35–40)

Thus, the riot ended before it had done any damage. The
town clerk had pointed out to the people what danger they
were in. We saw in the case of Antioch that the whole city
was responsible for any crimes committed during a riot, and
it could be very bad if the governor or the emperor himself
decided Ephesus needed to be taught a lesson. There are
official ways a citizen can bring charges against these Christians, he tells the people. So if they're really doing something wrong, the regular channels will take care of it.

Paul and the Ephesians

This priceless portrait of a city in commotion tells us a lot
about what life was like in Ephesus. The city was intensely
proud of its Wonder of the World, the Temple of Artemis. Tourism was also a big part of the local economy, and
people were constantly coming from all over to see the
famous sights. Thousands of people thought their prosperity depended on those sightseers.

It also tells us that Ephesus had a large and recognizable
Jewish community. There seems to have been some sim-
mering tension—Jews, after all, denied the existence of
Artemis of the Ephesians.

And finally, Luke's story tells us that Paul had been very successful in Ephesus—so successful that the souvenir salesmen thought their jobs were on the line. In Athens, Paul had been treated as an interesting crank with some new philosophy that might be fun to listen to. In Ephesus, he was building a Church.

Later, Paul would write a letter to that Church. His letter tells us that the Ephesian Church was made up mostly of Gentile converts: he tells them to remember that "you Gentiles in the flesh ... were at that time separated from Christ, alienated from the commonwealth of Israel, and strangers to the covenants of promise, having no hope and without God in the world" (2:11–12).

Some of Paul's most famous and beloved thoughts are in that letter, including the passage from chapter 5 that is read at many weddings: "He who loves his wife loves himself" (5:28). When we compare it to the letters to the Corinthians and the one to the Galatians, we get the impression that Paul wasn't nearly as worried about the Ephesians. The Church in Corinth seems to have been a problem child from the start, but Paul doesn't have to tell the Ephesians to knock it off and stop poking one another in the back seat.

We get the same impression from Saint Ignatius of Antioch, who also wrote a letter to the Church at Ephesus while he was on his way to Rome and martyrdom. He praises the Ephesians' faith over and over, mentioning in particular how they refused to listen to false teachers.

John and the Mother of God

Christian tradition tells us there were some false teachers to be found at Ephesus, but after the reign of Domitian, John the Apostle was there as well. He had been exiled to the Aegean island of Patmos, where tradition says he wrote the Book of Revelation. In the beginning of that book, the angel has a message for Ephesus, and John also mentions how the Ephesians refused to listen to false teachers, in particular the Nicolaitans. Eusebius tells us that John was recalled from Patmos after Domitian died, when the Roman Senate decreed a general return of the political exiles. He settled in Ephesus.

Saint Irenaeus passes on one story about John's time in Ephesus, told by John's disciple Polycarp, "whom I [Irenaeus] also saw in my early youth, for he lived a very long time". He continues, "And there are some who have been told by him, how John, the Lord's disciple, was in Ephesus, going to bathe; and when he saw Cerinthus in the place, he leaped out of the bath without using it, adding, 'Run away, or the bath itself might fall on us, since Cerinthus, the enemy of the truth, is in it.'"[2]

Ephesus was a good place to take a bath, by the way. Its municipal water system was one of the best in the world, and there were several good public baths. As for Cerinthus, he seems to have been one of those Nicolaitans mentioned in the Book of Revelation, or someone who developed their doctrines into his own system.

Irenaeus also tells us that John wrote his Gospel while he was at Ephesus. Modern scholars debate whether John the Apostle was really the writer of that Gospel, but Irenaeus is not many steps away from the facts: Irenaeus knew Polycarp, and Polycarp knew John.

Because John was there, some traditions say that Mary, the Mother of the Lord, was with him. We remember that,

[2] Irenaeus, *Against Heresies* 3.3.4, trans. Alexander Roberts and William Rambaut, in *ANF*, vol. 1, ed. Alexander Roberts, James Donaldson, and A. Cleveland Coxe (Buffalo, N.Y.: Christian Literature Publishing, 1885), revised and edited for New Advent by Kevin Knight, http://www.newadvent.org/fathers/0103303.htm.

just before he died on the Cross, Jesus made John responsible for his mother (see Jn 19:26–27)—a very important
consideration in a society where a widow had few resources
if she didn't have a son to take care of her. Many traditions
say she was still in Jerusalem when she "fell asleep", but
in Ephesus, they believed that Mary had come there with
John. There's a house in the country outside the ruined city
that is shown to pilgrims as the House of the Virgin Mary.
Was it really? Some say yes and some say no. But what is
unquestionable is that the people of Ephesus became very
attached to the Blessed Virgin. As Ephesus became Christian, she replaced Artemis of the Ephesians as the protector
of the city.

Though John lived at Ephesus, tradition tells us the city's
first bishop was Saint Timothy, the friend and protégé of
Paul. Timothy was a Greek Jew who had been familiar
with Scripture since he was a child.

Ephesus is also the scene of Saint Justin Martyr's *Dialogue
with Trypho*. Justin was a Christian who put on the robes of
a philosopher and taught Christianity as the perfect form of
philosophy. In the dialogue, Justin has a friendly argument
with a Jewish philosophy student named Trypho. The dialogue ends without a dramatic conversion; instead, Trypho asks to be remembered as a friend, and Justin, about
to set sail from Ephesus, urges him to "believe that Jesus is
the Christ of God".[3]

Justin's dialogue tells us Ephesus was a place where the
Jewish community was prosperous and well educated.
Although most of the people Paul wrote to in the Letter
to the Ephesians had been Gentiles, tradition says several
of the earliest bishops were Jews.

[3] Justin, *Dialogue with Trypho* 142, trans. Marcus Dods and George Reith, in
ANF, vol. 1, ed. Alexander Roberts, James Donaldson, and A. Cleveland Coxe
(Buffalo, N.Y.: Christian Literature Publishing, 1885), revised and edited for
New Advent by Kevin Knight, http://www.newadvent.org/fathers/01289.htm.

The Council of Ephesus

The Church in Ephesus grew to be one of the most influential in the eastern Mediterranean world. It claimed authority over all the churches in Asia, meaning the Roman Diocese of Asia. As the power of Constantinople grew, Ephesus held on to its own prestige and was inclined to side with the opposition if there was any dispute that put the bishop of Constantinople on one side. The biggest of those disputes came up in the year 431, when Nestorius became bishop of Constantinople.

We remember from our visit to Alexandria how Nestorius created a big stir in the Church with his supposed technical distinctions about the Mother of God. According to the historian Socrates Scholasticus, the trouble started with a priest named Anastasius, who had come with Nestorius from Antioch and who was one of the new bishop's most trusted advisers. One day, Anastasius was preaching in the church, and he said, "Let no one call Mary 'Mother of God': for Mary was only a woman, and it is impossible that God should be born of a woman."[4] "These words created a great sensation", Socrates says, "and troubled many both of the clergy and laity. Up to now they had been taught to acknowledge Christ as God, and by no means to separate his humanity from his divinity on account of the economy of incarnation."[5]

Nestorius thought highly of Anastasius, so he defended his priest in his own sermons. Nestorius was also the sort of preacher who liked to make fussy technical distinctions. He said you could call Mary Mother of the Christ

[4] Socrates Scholasticus, *Ecclesiastical History* 7.32, trans. A. C. Zenos, in *NPNF*, 2nd series, vol. 2, ed. Philip Schaff and Henry Wace (Buffalo: Christian Literature Publishing, 1890), revised and edited for New Advent by Kevin Knight, http://www.newadvent.org/fathers/26017.htm.
[5] Ibid.

(*Christotokos* in Greek), but *technically* you couldn't call her
Mother of God (*Theotokos*).

"The general impression", Socrates says, "was that
Nestorius was tainted with the errors of Paul of Samosata
and Photinus, and wanted to foist on the church the blas-
phemous dogma that the Lord is a mere man."[6]

Socrates adds that these accusations were probably unfair
to Nestorius, but Nestorius brought them on himself by
misunderstanding what he was preaching. Socrates gives
us a character study of Nestorius that shows a man whose
fatal flaw was proud self-confidence:

> Having myself perused the writings of Nestorius, I shall
> candidly express my own beliefs about him: and as I have
> already, with no personal antipathies at all, mentioned his
> faults, I shall likewise be unbiased by the accusations of
> his adversaries to detract from his merits. I cannot then
> concede either that he was a follower of the heretics with
> whom he was thus classed, or that he denied the Divinity
> of Christ: but he seemed scared at the term Theotokos as
> though it were some terrible phantom. The fact is, the
> causeless alarm he manifested on this subject just exposed
> his grievous ignorance: for instead of being a man of
> learning, as his natural eloquence caused him to be con-
> sidered, he was in reality disgracefully illiterate. Because
> he could express himself so easily, he had contempt for
> the drudgery of an accurate examination of the ancient
> expositors, and he was puffed up with a vain confidence
> in his own powers.[7]

Nestorius seems to have been puffed up with enough
confidence to think a council of the Church would confirm

[6] Ibid.
[7] Ibid.

his beliefs. But some of his confidence evaporated when
he heard that the council would be held at Ephesus. Ephesus! The city where Mary spent her last days. The city that
just might be more enthusiastic than any other about the
Mother of God. We get the impression that Nestorius was
a bit worried, not only about the outcome of the council, but also about his physical safety. "Immediately after
Easter, therefore," says Socrates, "Nestorius, escorted by a
strong body of his adherents, went to Ephesus, and found
many prelates already there."[8]

Nestorius was counting on support from some of his
old friends from Antioch. But John, the current bishop of
Antioch, was delayed, along with a number of the other
Eastern bishops. As we remember from our visit to Alexandria, Cyril, bishop of Alexandria and the chief opponent
of Nestorius, had been made president of the council. Following the emperor's schedule to the letter, he convened
the council before John and the others arrived. Nestorius
refused to consider the council in session until his friends
from the East were there. The result was that the meeting
was made up of Cyril and his supporters, so by the time
the Easterners got there, Nestorius had already been condemned and deposed.

John was furious when he found out he had been left
out. He convened a counter-council, which condemned
and deposed Cyril. Cyril and his supporters deposed John.
(John and Cyril would be reconciled later.)

Too late, Nestorius decided it wasn't worth fussing over
technical terms, as Socrates tells us: "When Nestorius saw
that the contention which had been raised was thus tend-
ing to schism and the destruction of communion, in bitter
regret he cried out: 'Let Mary be called Mother of God,

[8] Ibid., 7.34.

if you will, and let all disputing cease.' But although he made this recantation, no notice was taken of it; for his deposition was not revoked, and he was banished to Oasis, where he still remains."[9]

The Oasis was a habitable spot in the remote Egyptian desert where the most intractable and dangerous people were sent to get them out of the way. When Socrates was writing, Nestorius was still there. He lived some time, writing his memoirs, which were rediscovered in the 1800s. It turns out he thought life was unfair.

Two more councils would be held at Ephesus, but they're not considered real councils by Catholic and Orthodox Christians. The Second Council of Ephesus was notoriously called the "robber council" by Saint Leo the Great.

In the later 400s, Ephesus was largely destroyed in one of the many wars that ravaged the Roman Empire. It never recovered. When the Crusaders came centuries later, they expected to find a thriving city and instead found a few scraggly huts. Today the site has been excavated, and we can see enough of the remains to get some idea of how the people of Ephesus lived when the city was rich and bustling.

But Ephesus is gone. As with every one of the churches mentioned at the beginning of the Book of Revelation, its lampstand has been removed.

---

[9] Ibid.

6

Edessa

King Abgar was a sick man, and the best doctors in the world couldn't do a thing for him. But there were stories circulating about a man in Judea who could cure anything—even death. Desperate for help, the king wrote—or dictated—a letter and sent it off to Jerusalem in the hands of his most trusted minister, a man named Hannan, who was also his archivist and chief painter:

> Abgar Ukkama, to Jesus, the Good Physician, who has appeared in the country of Jerusalem. My Lord: Peace. I have heard of you and of your healing, that it is not by medicines and roots that you heal, but by your word you open the eyes of the blind, you make the lame to walk, cleanse the lepers, and make the deaf to hear. And unclean spirits and lunatics, and those tormented, you heal them by your word; you also raise the dead. And when I heard of these great wonders you do, I decided in my mind that either you are God, who have come down from heaven and do these things, or you are the Son of God, who do all these things. Therefore, I have written to request of you to come to me who adore you, and to heal the disease I have, as I believe in you. This also I have heard, that the Jews murmur against you and persecute you, and even seek to crucify you, and contemplate treating you cruelly. I possess one small and

beautiful city, and it is big enough for both of us to live in it in peace.[1]

Hannan found the famous Jesus staying at the house of Gamaliel, the chief priest of the Jews. When Jesus received the letter, he said:

> Go and say to your lord, who has sent you to me, "Blessed are you, who, although you have not seen me, believe in me, for it is written of me, Those who see me will not believe in me, and those who do not see me will believe in me. But as to what you have written to me, that I should come to you, that for which I was sent here is now finished, and I am going up to my Father, who sent me, and when I have gone up to him, I will send you one of my disciples, who will cure the disease you have, and restore you to health; and he will convert everyone with you to everlasting life. Your city shall be blessed, and no enemy shall again become master of it forever."[2]

Hannan wrote down Jesus' words. Then, being a skillful painter, he whipped out his brush and paintbox and painted a lifelike portrait of Jesus to bring back to the king.

> And when Abgar the king saw the likeness, he received it with great joy, and placed it with great honor in one of his palatial houses. Hannan, the keeper of the archives, related to him everything which he had heard from Jesus, as His words were put by him in writing.[3]

After Jesus had ascended to heaven, his promise was kept. The Apostle Thomas sent Thaddeus, or Addai, one

---

[1] George Phillips, ed. and trans., *The Doctrine of Addai, the Apostle* (London: Trübner, 1876), https://www.tertullian.org/fathers/addai_2_text.htm.
[2] Ibid.
[3] Ibid.

of the seventy who had been sent out by Jesus, to heal Abgar's disease, and Thaddeus taught the Way to Abgar and all his people.

The Letters in the Archives

This is the story the people of Edessa believed about the beginning of Christianity in their city. The version we've just heard comes from the *Doctrine of Addai, the Apostle*, a Syriac document that most scholars today date to about 400. But we know the basic story is much older than that. We find it in the writings of the Greek-speaking historian Eusebius, who wrote almost a century earlier and gives us similar wording for the correspondence between Abgar and Jesus, although his version doesn't include the prophecy that the city will never be conquered.

That prophecy, however, would become one of the great treasures of the city. As we'll see later, the people of Edessa inscribed it on the city gates, and they relied on it as their main defense.

The things people believe—as we've seen more than once—tell us a lot about history, even if the things themselves aren't true. In this case, the fact that people in Edessa believed their king had corresponded with Christ himself and that they pointed to the documents in the archives as proof shows that they believed their Christianity was very ancient. It wouldn't have been possible for them to believe that unless there had been Christians in Edessa for quite a long time—at the very least, longer than anyone alive could remember, and probably longer than their parents or grandparents could remember.

Eusebius tells us the correspondence could be found in the archives at Edessa:

You have written evidence of these things taken from the
archives of Edessa, which was at that time a royal city. For
in the public registers there, which contain accounts of
ancient times and the acts of Abgar, these things have been
found preserved down to the present time. But there is no
better way than to hear the epistles themselves, which we
have taken from the archives and have literally translated
from the Syriac language.[4]

Eusebius doesn't usually lie about his sources, so we can
believe him when he says the letters were in the archives at
Edessa. That doesn't prove, of course, that they were really
what they claimed to be; it just proves that, in the early 300s,
people in Edessa *believed* they had correspondence between
Jesus and King Abgar in their archives. In this case, we
have independent confirmation: in the late 300s,[5] a woman
named Egeria, or Etheria, from the West (probably what is
now Portugal or France) wrote a journal of her pilgrimage
to the East, a trip that included Edessa, where she also saw
the letters between Abgar and Jesus. "The letter is kept
with great reverence at the city of Edessa", she reports.[6]

Eusebius doesn't mention the picture painted by Hannan. That picture would later become a big part of the
legend. In later versions, it was a miraculous image made
without hands, and it was one of the chief glories of
the city. Later it was moved to Constantinople, where
it stayed till 1204, when the Crusaders from the West

---

[4] Eusebius, *Church History* 1.13.5, trans. Arthur Cushman McGiffert, in
NPNF, 2nd series, vol. 1, ed. Philip Schaff and Henry Wace (Buffalo, N.Y.:
Christian Literature Publishing, 1890), revised and edited for New Advent by
Kevin Knight, http://www.newadvent.org/fathers/250101.htm.

[5] The date is uncertain; some scholars say the middle 400s.

[6] M. L. (Herbert) McClure and Charles Lett Feltoe, trans. and eds., *The Pilgrimage of Etheria* (London: Society for Promoting Christian Knowledge; New
York: Macmillan, 1919), p. 30.

sacked the city and looted everything portable. It may have gone back to France; a relic there was identified with the miraculous image of Edessa. If so, it was lost during the French Revolution.

If Abgar (historians know him as Abgar V) really did become a Christian, then his successors lapsed back into paganism. Nevertheless, Christianity took firm root there before the time of Constantine, so that Eusebius, writing in the early 300s, could end the story of Abgar by saying, "And even to this day, the whole city of Edessa is devoted to the name of Christ."[7]

Edessa in Christian History

Edessa was a city at the eastern edge of the Roman Empire, not far from the border with the powerful Persian, or Parthian, empire. Today it's still an important city in Turkey, now called Urfa.

Ancient Edessenes mostly spoke Syriac, a language we've heard about before. Syriac began as the Edessene dialect of Aramaic, the language Jesus and his disciples spoke in everyday life. Through the influence of Edessa, the Syriac language would become to the Eastern Church what Latin is to the Western Church—the universal language of religion and literature. Churches as far away as southern India used Syriac as the language of the liturgy.

One of the first big names in Edessa's Christian history is Bardaisan, a Gnostic heretic who founded a sect known as the Bardaisanites. Bardaisan died in 222. Although he was a heretic, his influence on Edessa's Christian culture was big. He was especially famous for his hymns in the Syriac

---

[7] Eusebius, *Church History* 2.1.7, http://www.newadvent.org/fathers/250102.htm.

language, and (as we'll see) conveying theology through song would be an important part of the Edessene Christian tradition. A later Orthodox theologian was forced to admit Bardaisan had talent: "Ye sons of the good [God], pray for Bardaisan, for in his heathenism there went a Legion in his heart but our Lord in his mouth."[8] That praise came from Saint Ephrem the Syrian, and we'll meet him in just a moment.

Edessa suffered greatly in the persecution of Diocletian, the last and worst of the persecutions. As the historian J. B. Segal points out, the struggle was not just between Christian and pagan, but between Edessenes and their Roman rulers.[9] If Eusebius is right about the city being mostly Christian in his time, then the Christian population in Edessa was already large by the time of Diocletian. The martyrologies tell us that pagan and Jewish inhabitants of the city also paid their respects to the courage of the martyrs. Edessa might belong to the Roman Empire, but it remembered when it was its own kingdom, and it kept an independent streak.

In fact, as a Christian center, Edessa got a big boost from one of the greatest disasters to the Roman Empire. We've heard about Julian the Apostate before. He was the emperor who tried to take the Roman Empire back to his fantasy of the pagan good old days. He led an army into Persia and at first had some success, but the Persians wore him down, and at last he was killed far inside enemy territory. The soldiers picked Jovian as his successor, and Jovian made a disastrous deal with the Persians that gave up all Rome's easternmost provinces in exchange for the Persians letting his army out alive.

[8] Saint Ephrem the Syrian, quoted in J. B. Segal, *Edessa, "The Blessed City"* (Oxford: Clarendon Press, 1970), p. 36.

[9] J. B. Segal, *Edessa, "The Blessed City"* (Oxford: Clarendon Press, 1970), p. 86.

One of the cities in those provinces was Nisibis, the great fortress of the Eastern Roman Empire and an important center of Christianity. The Christian citizens of Nisibis were forced to pack up and leave on short notice. Many settled in Edessa, including one who would come to be known as the most important theologian and writer in Syriac Christianity: Saint Ephrem, known in the West as Saint Ephrem the Syrian.

Ephrem the Syrian

The thing that made Ephrem so popular was that he made theology fun. Other Christians wrote tracts carefully explaining the truth to the intellectuals who could read and understand them. Ephrem set the truth to music, so you could walk down the street singing it. With a true poet's sense of metaphor, he could look at a pearl and see the whole mystery of the Incarnation.

> What are you like? Let your stillness speak to one who hears you. Talk to us with your silent mouth. Whoever hears your halting silence sees the image of our Redeemer....
>
> Your mother is a virgin of the sea.... Your fair conception was without seed, and your generation without intercourse, and your birth without brothers....
>
> Your beauty is a shadowy image of the beauty of the Son, who clothed himself with suffering when the nails passed through him. They handled you roughly when the awl passed through you, just as they did his hands. And because of his sufferings, he was a king; just as because of your sufferings, your beauty is increased.[10]

[10] Ephrem the Syrian, *The Pearl*, Rhythm the Second, in *Select Works of S. Ephrem the Syrian*, trans. J. B. Morris (Oxford: John Henry Parker, 1847).

Saint Ephrem got himself noticed among the Greek-speaking Christians too. Here's what the ancient Greek-speaking historian Sozomen has to say about him.

> Ephrem the Syrian was entitled to the highest honors, and was the greatest ornament of the church. He was a native of Nisibis, or of the neighboring territory. He devoted his life to monastic philosophy; and although he received no instruction, he became, contrary to all expectation, so proficient in the learning and language of the Syrians, that he comprehended with ease the most abstruse theorems of philosophy. His style of writing was so full of splendid oratory and sublimity of thought that he surpassed all the writers of Greece. If the works of those Greek writers were to be translated into Syriac, or any other language, and the beauties of the Greek language taken away from them, they would keep little of their original elegance and value. Ephraim's productions do not have this disadvantage: they were translated into Greek during his life, and translations are even now being made, and yet they preserve much of their original force and power, so that his works are not less admired when read in Greek than when read in Syriac. Basil, who was subsequently bishop of the metropolis of Cappadocia, was a great admirer of Ephraim, and was astonished at his erudition. I think the opinion of Basil, who was the most learned and eloquent man of his age, is a stronger testimony to the merit of Ephraim than anything that could be written in his praise.[11]

Relying on the Prophecy

Since it was near the eastern frontier, Edessa was always in danger from any ambitious Persian emperor who wanted

[11] Sozomen, *Ecclesiastical History* 3.16, trans. Edward Walford, in *The Ecclesiastical History of Sozomen: Comprising a History of the Church from A.D. 324 to A.D. 440*, by Sozomen and Photius I, Patriarch of Constantinople (London: Henry G. Bohn, 1855).

to teach the Romans a lesson. More than once the city was besieged. The historian Procopius tells us that the anti-Christian emperor Chosroes went after Edessa specifically because of the prophecy that said no enemy would ever take it: "Then a sort of ambition came over Chosroes to capture the city of Edessa. For he was led on to this by a saying of the Christians, and it kept irritating his mind, because they maintained that it could not be taken, for the following reason."[12]

From here Procopius gives us the story of Abgar, including the correspondence with Jesus:

> When the Christ saw this message, he wrote in reply to Abgar, saying distinctly that he would not come, but promising him health in the letter. And they say that he added this also, that never would the city be liable to capture by the barbarians. This final portion of the letter was entirely unknown to those who wrote the history of that time; for they did not even make mention of it anywhere; but the people of Edessa say that they found it with the letter, so that they have even caused the letter to be inscribed in this form on the gates of the city instead of any other defense.[13]

This account is all the more interesting because the sober and unsuperstitious Procopius doesn't really believe the legend: "And the thought once occurred to me that, if Christ did not write this thing just as I have told it, still, since people have come to believe in it, Christ wishes to guard the city uncaptured for this reason, so that he may never give them any pretext for error. As for these things, then, let them be as God wills, and so let them be told."[14]

[12] Procopius, *History of the Wars* 2.12.6–7, trans. H.B. Dewing, in *Procopius* (Cambridge, Mass.: Harvard University Press, 1914).

[13] Ibid., 2.12.25–26.

[14] Ibid., 2.12.30.

As Procopius tells us, Chosroes failed—more than once. The city still had not been taken in the middle 500s, when Procopius was writing.

But whether it was divine or just lucky, the city's protection would not last forever. Like the rest of the Christian East, Edessa fell under Muslim domination. It was a frequent flash point for battles between Christian and Muslim powers, and it became the center of one of the Crusader states in the late Middle Ages. The city still had a large Christian population until the twentieth century, when most of the Christians were driven out by massacres and political changes.

Today Urfa is known as one of the most religious cities in Turkey, but the religion is Islam. The influence of ancient Edessa, however, continues to be felt throughout the Christian East, where Syriac is still the language of Christianity. And wherever in the world Syriac Christians have gone, they have brought with them the glorious tradition of Edessa, the Blessed City.

7

Lugdunum

We've spent a lot of time in the East as we explored the great cities of early Christian history. Today we're going back to the West, all the way to the capital of Gaul—Lugdunum, today's Lyon. But, as we'll see, we're taking some of the East with us.

Today Lyon is the second city of France, at least in terms of metropolitan population. Lugdunum was hardly less important in its own time. What makes the city so important, then and now, is its location. It's about two hundred miles up the Rhône from the Mediterranean—but the river is navigable all the way. That makes it the natural point where everything from the interior of Gaul collects for shipment out to the rest of the world and where everything coming into Gaul pauses before it goes on its way.

A city with that advantage attracted traders, and the thriving economy attracted every other kind of people. You could see everyone from everywhere in Lugdunum. In particular, it had a large population of Greek speakers from Asia Minor in the eastern half of the empire, and it was probably among those Greek speakers that Christianity first took root.

We don't know when the Good News first came to Lugdunum. It's likely, though, that it was very soon after

Christianity started to spread. With so many people passing through the city from all parts of the Roman world, some of the very earliest Christians must have reached the place.

Christians made up a small group for a while. But by the middle of the 100s, the Church in Lugdunum was big enough to need its own bishop, Pothinus, who was sent there by Saint Polycarp, the disciple of John the Apostle. The Christian community continued to grow until the year 177, when the Church in Lugdunum suddenly got some very unwelcome attention.

Blandina and the Martyrs of Lugdunum

Under the virtuous Stoic philosopher-emperor Marcus Aurelius, persecutions increased—whether because of the emperor or in spite of him is still up for debate. One of the persecutions we happen to know about in detail was the one in Lugdunum, because the Church in Gaul sent a circular letter to the churches in the East detailing the heroism of the martyrs. Most of that letter still survives, thanks to the Church historian Eusebius, who loved original sources more than any other ancient historian.

Eusebius introduces the story by giving us the geographical setting.

The country in which the Christians would be led to the theater was Gaul, of which Lugdunum and Vienna were the principal and most celebrated cities. The Rhône passes through both of them, flowing in a broad stream through the entire region.

We should note, by the way, that the Vienna mentioned here is not the famous one in Austria but a smaller city about twenty miles south of Lugdunum. It's called Vienne today, and it still preserves its Roman theater and other landmarks from ancient times.

From here Eusebius gives us the text of the letter sent by the surviving Christians—or at least most of it: he summarizes parts he thinks are not as relevant to the story. But what he has preserved is a very detailed account of one of the early persecutions. This is how it begins: "The servants of Christ residing at Vienna and Lugdunum, in Gaul, to the brethren throughout Asia and Phrygia, who hold the same faith and hope of redemption, peace and grace and glory from God the Father and Christ Jesus our Lord".[1]

We note that the letter is sent specifically to the Christians of Asia and Phrygia—places in the East from which many of the Christians of Lugdunum had come. It suggests that the Church in Lugdunum considered itself a daughter church of these Eastern churches. The writers tell us that things were suddenly very bad for the Christians:

> The greatness of the tribulation in this region, and the fury of the heathen against the saints, and the sufferings of the blessed witnesses, we cannot recount accurately, nor indeed could they possibly be recorded.
>
> For with all his might the adversary fell upon us, giving us a foretaste of his unbridled activity at his future coming. In every way he tried to stir up his servants against the servants of God, not only shutting us out from houses and baths and markets, but forbidding any of us to be seen anywhere at all.[2]

We don't know exactly what these new rules were that were such a burden to the Christians. We also don't know why the persecution came up at this time rather than any other, but the letter mentions that "they endured nobly the

[1] Eusebius, *Church History* 5, trans. Arthur Cushman McGiffert, in *NPNF*, 2nd series, vol. 1, ed. Philip Schaff and Henry Wace (Buffalo, N.Y.: Christian Literature Publishing, 1890), revised and edited for New Advent by Kevin Knight, http://www.newadvent.org/fathers/250101.htm.
[2] Ibid.

injuries heaped upon them by the populace: shouting and
blows and draggings and robberies and stonings and impris-
onments, and all things which an infuriated mob delight in
inflicting on enemies and adversaries."[3] So we can guess
there may have been an anti-Christian riot and the local
government responded by appeasing the mob and giving
them the show they wanted. The letter continues, "Then
they were taken to the forum by the tribune and the authorities of the city, and they were examined in the presence of
the whole multitude. And when they had confessed, they
were imprisoned until the arrival of the governor."[4]

The governor, the letter tells us, was equally inclined to
give the mob a good show and treated the accused with
cruelty and contempt. Under the torture, some of them
fell away and recanted their Christianity. "And some of
our heathen servants also were seized," the letter says,
"as the governor had commanded that all of us should be
examined publicly. These, being ensnared by Satan, and
fearing for themselves the tortures which they beheld the
saints endure, and being also urged on by the soldiers,
accused us falsely of Thyestean banquets and Œdipodean
intercourse"—in other words, cannibalism and incest, two
of the most common wild rumors about the Christians—
"and of deeds which are not only unlawful for us to speak
of or to think, but which we cannot believe were ever
done by human beings."[5]

This accusation made the mob even more furious, and
even the few friends the Christians had among the pagans
decided it wasn't safe to be their friends anymore.

From here the letter goes on to describe the sufferings
of the martyrs, who endured every torture the ingenuity

[3] Ibid.
[4] Ibid.
[5] Ibid.

of the enlightened Roman civilization could invent. Of all of them, though, the one who was remembered most was the young slave Blandina, "through whom", the letter says, "Christ showed that things which appear mean and obscure and despicable to men are with God of great glory, through love toward him manifested in power, and not boasting in appearance."[6] The letter continues:

> For while we all trembled, and [Blandina's] earthly mistress, who was herself also one of the witnesses, feared that on account of the weakness of [Blandina's] body, she would be unable to make bold confession, Blandina was filled with such power as to be delivered and raised above those who were torturing her by turns from morning till evening in every manner, so that they acknowledged that they were conquered, and could do nothing more to her. And they were astonished at her endurance, as her entire body was mangled and broken; and they testified that one of these forms of torture was sufficient to destroy life, not to speak of so many and so great sufferings.[7]

But the blessed woman, like a noble athlete, renewed her strength in her confession; and her comfort and recreation and relief from the pain of her sufferings was in exclaiming, "I am a Christian, and there is nothing vile done by us."[8]

The others endured similar treatment. Some of them died; some of them *should* have died but revived miraculously in prison. Pothinus, the aged bishop, was beaten and died soon after from the mistreatment.

At last the usual show was arranged: the Christians were to be torn to shreds by wild animals in the theater,

[6] Ibid.
[7] Ibid.
[8] Ibid.

for the delight and amusement of the good citizens. But, as the letter tells us, there were some disappointments in that show: "Blandina was suspended on a stake, and exposed to be devoured by the wild beasts who should attack her. And because she appeared as if hanging on a cross, and because of her earnest prayers, she inspired the combatants with great zeal. For they looked on her in her conflict, and beheld with their outward eyes, in the form of their sister, him who was crucified for them, that he might persuade those who believe on him, that everyone who suffers for the glory of Christ has fellowship always with the living God."[9] As none of the wild beasts at that time touched her, she was taken down from the stake and cast again into prison.

Tortures and trials went on for days. More Christians, inspired by the courage of the martyrs, confessed and were seized. At last Blandina's time for martyrdom came, as the letter tells us:

> After all these, on the last day of the contests, Blandina was again brought in, with Ponticus, a boy about fifteen years old.... Ponticus, encouraged by his sister so that even the heathen could see that she was confirming and strengthening him, having nobly endured every torture, gave up the ghost.
>
> But the blessed Blandina, last of all, having, as a noble mother, encouraged her children and sent them before her victorious to the King, endured herself all their conflicts and hastened after them, glad and rejoicing in her departure as if called to a marriage supper, rather than cast to wild beasts.
>
> And, after the scourging, after the wild beasts, after the roasting seat, she was finally enclosed in a net, and thrown

[9] Ibid.

before a bull. And having been tossed about by the animal, but feeling none of the things which were happening to her, on account of her hope and firm hold upon what had been entrusted to her, and her communion with Christ, she also was sacrificed. And the heathen themselves confessed that never among them had a woman endured so many and such terrible tortures.[10]

The cruelty did not end even after the martyrs were dead. The governor made sure the Christians would have no relics: the bodies were closely guarded, and then they were burned and the ashes swept into the Rhône.

This precious letter is one of the most detailed accounts we have of a Roman persecution. But it leaves out the name of probably the most famous Christian—aside from Blandina—who ever lived in Lugdunum. That's because he had been sent with a letter to Rome.

Irenaeus versus All the Heretics at Once

Irenaeus was a priest in Lugdunum when the persecution broke out. The Christians in prison sent him with a letter about the Montanist heretics in Lugdunum, hoping their present suffering would add authority to their words. What was their message? We don't know. That letter has been lost over the many centuries between them and us. But it did mean that Irenaeus was in Rome when the news came that Pothinus, the bishop, had died. Who would replace him? Here was an obvious candidate. Irenaeus was sent back as bishop, and his first duty would be to mop up after the persecution.

[10] Ibid.

Who was this Irenaeus? Like Pothinus, he had come from Asia Minor. When he was young, Irenaeus had known Saint Polycarp, a disciple of the Apostle John.

> I remember where Polycarp used to sit when he taught. I remember the places he used to go, how he lived, what he looked like, the speeches he made to the crowds, the things he told us about his conversation with John and others who saw the Lord; how he remembered their sayings, and what he heard from them about the Lord, about his power and teaching; repeating the precepts, and everything that matched Holy Scripture—out of the mouths (as I said) of those who themselves had seen the Word of Life in the flesh with their own eyes.[11]

What this means was that Irenaeus was two steps away from Jesus himself. Jesus, John, Polycarp, Irenaeus—that was the chain of tradition.

He knew Polycarp in Smyrna, the city in Asia Minor. How did Irenaeus get to Gaul? Some scholars think he was sent there by Polycarp himself, on the grounds that the Church in Lugdunum was a daughter church of the Church in Smyrna. Others think that Irenaeus was still in Smyrna when Polycarp was martyred and that he left for Gaul some time afterward. Either way, it seems to have been natural that the Church in Lugdunum would be looking eastward for priests. Of the martyrs mentioned by name in the letter Eusebius recorded for us, half have Greek names.

That still leaves half who were either native to Lugdunum or from elsewhere in the West, and that native element was growing. Irenaeus would have been able to get along well in Greek with a good number of the Christians

[11] Ibid.

and some of the traders who had settled in Lugdunum. But he would have had to learn Latin to make himself useful to the growing Church there. Years later, at the beginning of his magnum opus, he wrote, "You will not expect from me, living as I do among the Celts, and used to speaking a barbarous dialect most of the time, any display of rhetoric, which I have never learned."[12] He was writing in Greek, which was the language of educated people. Marcus Aurelius, the emperor during the persecution of the martyrs of Lugdunum, was a Westerner, but his famous book *Meditations* was written in Greek, because it was written for an educated audience. But in daily life, it was more and more necessary for Irenaeus to speak Latin as the Church grew.

The years after the spectacular persecution were years of peace for the most part. The Church grew rapidly in Lugdunum. With that rapid growth came the same problems other churches were having. Teachers who professed to be Christians were teaching radically different sorts of Christianity. In Irenaeus' time, they were mostly Gnostics.

Gnosticism is a kind of catch-all term for a range of beliefs that have the idea of secret knowledge at their core—thus the name, from the Greek word *gnosis*, meaning "knowledge". Christian Gnostics taught that there was one doctrine for the dull and stupid masses but that the real truth was reserved for us, the few insiders—and for you, if you pay your fees to the Gnostic teacher. (Irenaeus tells us specifically that the Gnostics' disciples had "to pay a high price for an acquaintance with such profound mysteries".[13])

---

[12] Irenaeus, *Against Heresies* 1, preface, 3, trans. Alexander Roberts and William Rambaut, in *ANF*, vol. 1, ed. Alexander Roberts, James Donaldson, and A. Cleveland Coxe (Buffalo, N.Y.: Christian Literature Publishing, 1885), revised and edited for New Advent by Kevin Knight, http://www.newadvent.org/fathers/0103100.htm.

[13] Ibid., 1.4.3, http://www.newadvent.org/fathers/0103104.htm.

This esoteric doctrine was expressed in impenetrable jargon that sure sounded impressive.

Faced with this problem, Irenaeus sat down to write one of the most ambitious works yet undertaken by a Christian thinker. He called it something like *So-Called Knowledge Refuted and Overturned*, but it's usually known as *Against Heresies*. It's nothing less than an encyclopedia of the various sects of Gnostics, along with Irenaeus' explanations of why they were wrong.

We can hardly admire Irenaeus enough merely for having the patience to wade through the pretentious meanderings of the Gnostics. Their tortuous mythology is full of Aeons and Proarches and generations and emanations and dozens of characters with symbolic names, and Irenaeus dutifully catalogues them all for us. But when he had to deal with Valentinus, his patience broke at last, and he was overcome by the most memorable fit of sarcasm in the history of early Christianity:

> Obviously, Valentinus himself is the one who was bold enough to come up with these names; so that, unless he had appeared in the world, the truth would still have been nameless. But if that's true, there's nothing to stop anyone else who deals with the same subjects from giving them names like this: There is a certain Proarche, royal, surpassing all thought, a power existing before every other substance, and extended into space in every direction. But along with it there exists a power which I term a Gourd; and along with this Gourd there exists a power which again I term Utter-Emptiness. This Gourd and Emptiness, since they are one, produced (and yet did not simply produce, so as to be apart from themselves) a fruit, everywhere visible, eatable, and delicious, which fruit-language calls a Cucumber. Along with this Cucumber exists a power of the same essence, which again I call a Melon. These

powers, the Gourd, Utter-Emptiness, the Cucumber, and the Melon, brought forth the remaining multitude of the delirious melons of Valentinus.[14]

Today Valentinus and his like are long forgotten, except by specialists in Christian history. You'll find many people who like to mourn the alternative Christianities supposedly suppressed by the early Church—which, as an illegal underground cult, hardly had the power to suppress anybody. But their enthusiasm usually wanes when they actually have to read what those Gnostics believed.

Saint Irenaeus set a high standard for bishops of Lugdunum. Some traditions say he died a martyr, but those are late and unreliable. He may have died of old age, but he was a tough act to follow. Nevertheless, in the centuries after him, we find a lot of bishops with "Saint" in front of their names. Irenaeus' successors were living up to their great model.

The city of Lugdunum suffered in the Dark Ages, like the rest of the cities of the West, but it survived better than most, and Charlemagne built it up into a famous center of learning. Today Lyon is littered with monuments of twenty centuries of Christian history, but perhaps no two figures are more celebrated than Saint Irenaeus, the great theologian, and Saint Blandina, the heroic martyr.

[14] Ibid., 1.11.4, http://www.newadvent.org/fathers/0103111.htm.

8

Ejmiatsin

We're heading back to the ancient East for our next city, but first we're going to stop in Venice in the early 1800s to visit with an Englishman for a while.

Today's Venice is one of the most expensive cities in the world, with its ancient landmarks scrupulously restored for the benefit of tourists and their cell-phone cameras. But in 1816, it was a city that had obviously seen better days. The Republic of Venice had come to an end in the Napoleonic wars nineteen years earlier, and Venice had been kicked around like a football in those wars until Napoleon was defeated in 1814, after which it was part of the Austrian Empire.

Mad, Bad, and Obsessed with Armenian

On the one hand, Venice was not rich anymore; on the other, it was full of decaying monuments of a glorious past when it had controlled practically the whole Mediterranean. It was just the sort of place to attract English travelers enamored with the Romantic movement in poetry and art, and it was full of aristocratic palaces they could rent for very little money.

It was just the place for the Romantic poet Lord Byron, who could no longer live in England because of the creditors who wanted to put him in prison and the husbands who wanted to kill him. "Mad, bad, and dangerous to know" was how one of his many Romantic conquests described him, but Byron was a brilliant poet and had a remarkably adaptable mind. He was always looking for something new to relieve his boredom, and in Venice he heard of the curious island monastery of San Lazzaro degli Armeni—Saint Lazarus of the Armenians. It was a tiny island, about a mile into the water, where Armenian Catholic monks lived.

Armenian? In Venice? Already it sounded mysterious and romantic. But when Byron visited and got to know the monks, he was suddenly obsessed with Armenian. He wrote to his friend Thomas Moore on December 5, 1816, "By way of divertisement, I am studying daily, at an Armenian monastery, the Armenian language. I found that my mind wanted something craggy to break upon; and this—as the most difficult thing I could discover here for an amusement—I have chosen, to torture me into attention."[1]

Byron did more than study the language. He helped one of the monks publish an Armenian and English grammar. He translated Armenian literature and translated some of his own poems into Armenian. All this was in spite of the fact that Armenian was not an easy language for Western Europeans to pick up casually. In his letter to Thomas Moore, Byron continues, "Four years ago the French instituted an Armenian professorship. Twenty pupils presented themselves on Monday

[1] George Gordon Byron, *Lord Byron's Armenian Exercises and Poetry* (Venice: In the island of S. Lazzaro, 1870), p. 10.

morning, full of noble ardour, ingenuous youth, and
impregnable industry. They persevered, with a courage worthy of the nation and of universal conquest, till
Thursday; when fifteen of the twenty succumbed to the
six-and-twentieth letter of the alphabet. It is, to be sure,
a Waterloo of an alphabet—that must be said for them."[2]
The twenty-sixth letter was only two-thirds of the way
through: the Armenian alphabet has thirty-eight letters.[3]
A Waterloo of an alphabet indeed!

Why was Byron suddenly so obsessed with Armenian?
What captured his notoriously flighty mind and made him
take lessons from monks, though Byron was certainly not
known for his religious enthusiasm? It seemed to Byron
that he had stumbled upon a lost civilization, a whole
continent of literature to explore that no one had ever
told him about before. "There are some very curious Mss.
in the monastery, as well as books; translations also from
Greek originals, now lost, and from Persian and Syriac
etc.; besides works of their own people."[4]

And that continent is still lost today for most of us. Specialists know there is a vast classical Armenian literature,
much of it still waiting to be explored by Westerners. But
most of the rest of us never think about Armenia. Most
of us are shocked to find out that Armenia was the first
Christian country on earth.

And this finally brings us to our famous ancient city
that most Americans have never heard of: Ejmiatsin (pro-
nounced "etch-myah-TSEEN"), also known as Vagharshapat ("vah-khar-sha-PAHT"), a city that for almost its
whole existence has had two names.

[2] Ibid., p. 12.
[3] P. Pascal Aucher, *A Grammar, Armenian and English* (Venice: Armenian
Press of St. Lazarus, 1832). This is the grammar Byron edited.
[4] Byron, *Armenian Exercises and Poetry*, p. 12.

Christianity Comes to Armenia

Armenia is a country that has always been stuck between empires. In the early Christian era, the empires were Rome and Parthia, whose constant bickering over their lengthy shared border made Armenia strategically important.

Most of the history of Armenia for the first three hundred years of the Christian era is the story of how Rome and Parthia fought for domination. Oddly, the Arsacid dynasty, which at least nominally ruled Armenia throughout that time, was a Parthian noble family but had been installed as rulers by the Romans.

In the year 258, King Chosroes, or Khosrov II, was assassinated by a Parthian named Anak, instigated by the Persian emperor, the Persians having replaced the Parthians as rulers of the empire to the east. In a furious rage, the Armenian nobles murdered Anak and his entire family—all but his baby son, Gregory, who was whisked away to Cappadocia in the Roman Empire.

Chosroes had only one heir, and he, too, was a baby—Tiridates, the third king of that name. With an infant king of Armenia, nothing could prevent the Persians from taking over Armenia. Just in time, Tiridates, too, was whisked out of Armenia. He ended up in the city of Rome.

Two children were orphaned at the same time—one the son of the assassin, the other the son of his victim. If we were writing a historical novel, we might be tempted to give them intertwined destinies. But then we would say, "No, that's too implausible. Nobody would believe it." History, however, is not limited by dramatic plausibility. If history wants to tie these children's destinies in knots, then that's what history will do.

Tiridates, the son of the king, was raised in Rome with every possible advantage. After all, he might be useful. Give

the Romans half a chance, and they would try to kick the
Persians out of Armenia. And they had the legitimate king
right here, ready to take his throne back if he had some help.
So Tiridates had the best possible education, and he grew
up multilingual and well versed in Roman military science.

Meanwhile, Gregory, the son of the assassin, was also
getting an education—but it was a different kind of education. He ended up in a Cappadocian family of Christians,
so he was brought up as a Christian.

Gregory would go on to become such an important
character in history that we don't know much about him.
We have stories galore, and many of them may be true.
But he was the kind of go-getter saint whose life accumu-
lates legends. We'll hear the stories as the Armenians have
always told them and then we'll try to sort out what we
really know.

The Romans had found their opportunity, and Tiridates, the exiled king, was back on the throne as a loyal
Roman ally. He brought with him a talented Armenian
who, like him, had been raised in the Roman Empire
and gave him an important government position. But this
other young Armenian turned out to be trouble for Tiridates. When Tiridates ordered him to worship a statue of
the local goddess Anahit, this young man refused.

"You've served me loyally for years", said Tiridates.
"Why do you refuse this one thing now?" "I've served
you as God tells us to serve our earthly masters", the man
explained. "But I can worship only God." He told Tiridates to give up his stubborn attachment to mere images
and worship the true God. Tiridates was furious. "You've
insulted me *and* the gods", he said. He had the man thrown
into prison and tortured. Then, at just the right dramatic
moment, one of the other men of the court recognized
that this Christian was none other than Gregory, son of

the man who had assassinated Tiridates' father. That did
not make Tiridates any less angry. According to the story,
he threw Gregory into a deep pit and left him there for
thirteen years—others say fifteen—and had him tortured
the whole time.[5]

Meanwhile, back in the Roman Empire, the emperor
Diocletian was looking for a wife. He hired a bunch of
portrait painters to go all through the empire to find the
most beautiful women and paint their portraits so that he
could look through them and pick out a wife for himself. It
turned out the most beautiful woman in the whole empire
was a Christian nun. Diocletian immediately started his
great persecution of the Christian churches in order to
show her that she had better marry him.

The intended bride and her sister nuns decided to run
far away, and they ended up in Ejmiatsin. But the king
there was a loyal ally of Diocletian. When Diocletian sent
to get his bride back, Tiridates found out how beautiful
she was, and he fell for her too. He tried to seduce her,
but nothing he could do would prevail. The furious king
had her killed, along with the other nuns and many other
Christians. This was such a wicked deed that the next time
Tiridates went hunting, he suddenly went mad and fell
from his chariot. Some versions of the story say he turned
into a boar. Thus, he learned the lesson every Catholic
bishop knows by heart: you don't mess with nuns.

The king's sister, however, started having visions. They
told her that only the Christian Gregory could put the king
back in his right mind. And so it happened. Gregory was

---

[5] The stories of Tiridates and Gregory are retold from Agathangelos. R. W.
Thomson, "Agathangelos", in *Encyclopædia Iranica* (London: Encyclopædia
Iranica Foundation, 1982–), vol. I, fasc. 6, pp. 607–8; article originally published December 15, 1984; online edition, 2011, http://www.iranicaonline.org
/articles/agathangelos.

brought up out of the pit, still miraculously alive after all
these years, and he cured the king's madness and his boor-
ishness. With such a powerful demonstration of the mercy
of God, Tiridates was convinced and became a Christian,
and all his people with him.

That's the story. Most modern historians would say it's
heavily embroidered with legend. They don't believe the
part about the king turning into a boar, for example.

Founding a Christian Literature

But strip away all the legend, and the facts are still amazing. Tiridates and Gregory are real historical figures. And
somehow Tiridates was converted to Christianity by Gregory. They call him Gregory the Illuminator, the Apostle
of Armenia. Since it happened before Rome became officially Christian, Armenia has the honor of being the first
Christian nation on earth.

It also has the honor of having what is probably the oldest Christian cathedral on earth. Ejmiatsin Cathedral was
originally built under King Tiridates III in the early 300s.
Most of it was destroyed by a Persian invasion in the late
400s, but it was rebuilt. Since then it has been gradually
expanded and adorned but never replaced. Today it is still
the seat of the Armenian Apostolic Church.

So the king was a Christian, and his capital had a fine
cathedral—all before the Roman Empire had become officially Christian. But there was a difficulty. What do you
do if your country is committed to Christianity, but all the
Christian literature is in a language most people who live
there don't understand? Well, you translate it. But in order
to have a literature at all, you first have to be able to write.
And although there are some indications that Armenian

had already been written down in some way, Armenia didn't really have a literate culture.

It was up to Armenia's next great cultural hero, Saint Mesrop Mashtots, to make Armenian literacy possible. Mesrop was a well-educated nobleman who was the official secretary of the king. In those days—about the year 400—Armenian royal business was written down in Greek and Persian, the languages of the two bordering empires. When Armenian had to be written at all, it seems, people borrowed one of the other writing systems—Greek or Persian or even Syriac—and tried to make the letters fit the sounds of their language. But their language had more sounds than there were letters in any of those alphabets.

After some years in court, Mesrop felt called to an ascetic life. He left the court, took holy orders, and went into a monastery. But after a few years of that, he came back out into public life again—this time as an evangelist.

As he traveled the country, making converts of the remaining pagans, he felt more and more the need to be able to record Christian truth in a language the people could understand. So, with the help of some other intellectual types, both in Armenia and abroad, he created an alphabet that would represent all the sounds of the Armenian language. His alphabet had thirty-six letters; two more were added during the Middle Ages, making the thirty-eight that Byron had to learn.

Once Armenian had an alphabet, the Armenian monks immediately set to translating all the important Christian literature into Armenian. First came the Holy Scriptures, of course. After that, the acts of the ecumenical councils were translated, as well as the liturgy—the Armenians had been using the Syriac liturgy until that time.

But they didn't stop with the basics. Mesrop sent Armenian monks to the great cities of the Greek-speaking

Eastern Roman Empire to study Greek and to bring back translations of as many good books as they could get their hands on.

For specialists in early Christianity, this makes a knowledge of Armenian essential. Once Lord Byron opened the floodgates, Western Europeans started to discover that countless important works thought to have been lost were still preserved in Armenian translations. Because of the tireless Armenian translators, we have added many previously lost works back into the canon of the Church Fathers. Over and over, as we go through the list of their writings, we come across the same kind of statement: the Greek original of this book has been lost, but it's preserved in an Armenian translation.

The Armenian Church separated from the Catholic and Orthodox churches, along with many of the Eastern churches that Westerners have traditionally called "monophysite", meaning they believe that Christ has one nature that is both divine and human, as opposed to the Catholic doctrine that the divine and human natures are distinct and unconfused but united in the one indivisible Son of God. These churches usually prefer to be called "miaphysite", one nature.

Armenian literature had its ups and downs, but Armenian art and writing flourished in the Middle Ages and has continued straight through to the present. In the 1500s, Armenia was conquered by the Persians, and many Armenian intellectuals left for Western Europe—just as the age of printing began. They brought their books with them and set up Armenian presses in Europe. Most Western Europeans ignored them, but they were preserving Armenian literature at a critical time.

A large number of Armenians once lived in what is today's Turkey under the Ottoman Empire, but during the

First World War and the wars that followed the collapse of the Ottoman government, somewhere around a million of them were massacred. The Armenian genocide is often the only thing the average American history student knows about Armenians. Today only about a hundred thousand Armenians live in Turkey, but they still make up the largest single group of Christians.

Today Armenia is an independent nation again since the fall of the Soviet Union. Its border with Turkey—just a few miles away from Ejmiatsin—is closed. Turkey has always officially denied the Armenian genocide and aggressively threatens institutions that mount exhibits or publish histories dealing with it. But in 1999, Turkey dedicated a towering memorial to the martyred Turks massacred by Armenians. It's the tallest monument in Turkey.

As for the city of Ejmiatsin, it's become a suburb of the current capital, Yerevan. But for Armenian Christians, Holy Ejmiatsin is still the spiritual capital of the Armenian Apostolic Church.

9

Constantinople

It wasn't enough to be the first Christian emperor. It wasn't enough to make Christianity the favored religion of the imperial government. Constantine also had to move the capital away from Rome. He took a look at the obscure Greek city of Byzantium and said to himself, "This is the place."

The Perfect Capital

It was geography that made Byzantium—soon to be named Constantinople, after you-know-who—such a perfect capital. A military leader like Constantine always asks first, "Can I defend this place?" The answer for Constantinople was an emphatic yes. It is surrounded on three sides by water. The land side is relatively narrow, and a general like Constantine would immediately think, "I can build a wall across that."

But being defensible is only part of what made Constantinople a perfect capital city. There are plenty of defensible mountaintops in the middle of nowhere, but Constantinople was in the middle of everywhere. Every ship going from the Black Sea to the Mediterranean had to pass right by Constantinople. It was close enough to mount an expedition to the eastern frontier, where the troublesome war with the Persians and the Parthians had been going on for hundreds of years. But it was not close enough to be in serious danger from the Parthians or Persians, or whoever was in charge over there at the moment.

Before Constantine, Byzantium was never more than moderately important, although it did have the advantage of being able to tax commerce going through the Bosporus between the Mediterranean and the Black Sea. But Constantine had more than one reason for putting his new capital there. First, there was the strategic importance of the place. It was also true that the eastern half of the empire had most of the population and most of the important cities, so governing it all from the West was inefficient. And then there was the fact that the aristocracy in the city of Rome was stubbornly pagan (and indeed would remain so for another century). By moving his capital to a newly founded city, Constantine could refound the empire on a Christian basis, with a capital city that was obviously Christian.

It took a lot of ambition to move the capital of the Roman world, but Constantine *had* a lot of ambition. The historian Socrates Scholasticus, who was a lifelong resident of Constantinople, tells us the new capital was Constantine's first priority after the Council of Nicaea.

After the synod, the emperor spent some time in recreation, and after the public celebration of his twentieth anniversary of his accession, he immediately devoted himself to repairing the churches of the city. This he carried into effect in other cities as well. He also enlarged the new capital, surrounded it with massive walls, and adorned it with various edifices. Having rendered it equal to imperial Rome, he named it Constantinople, establishing by law that it should be designated New Rome. This law was engraved on a pillar of stone erected in public view in the Strategium, near the emperor's equestrian statue.

In the same city, he also built two churches. One he named "Irene" and the other "The Apostles". According to Socrates Scholasticus, "Nor did he only improve the affairs of the Christians, as I have said, but he also destroyed the superstition of the heathens; for he brought forth their images into public view to ornament the city of Constantinople, and set up the Delphic tripods publicly in the Hippodrome."[1]

Eusebius, who knew Constantine and was a big fan of the emperor, tells us more about the magnificence of New Rome:

> Being fully resolved to distinguish the city which bore his name with especial honor, he embellished it with numerous sacred edifices, both memorials of martyrs on the largest scale, and other buildings of the most splendid kind, not only within the city itself, but in its vicinity: and thus at the same time he rendered honor to the memory of the martyrs, and consecrated his city to the martyrs' God. Being filled, too, with Divine wisdom, he determined to purge the city which was to be distinguished by his own name from idolatry of every kind, that henceforth no statues might be worshipped there in the temples of those falsely reputed to be gods, nor any altars defiled by the pollution of blood: that there might be no sacrifices consumed by fire, no demon festivals, nor any of the other ceremonies usually observed by the slaves of superstition.
>
> On the other hand one might see the fountains in the midst of the forum graced with figures representing

[1] Socrates Scholasticus, *Ecclesiastical History* 1.16, trans. A. C. Zenos, in *Nicene and Post-Nicene Fathers*, 2nd series, vol. 2, ed. Philip Schaff and Henry Wace (Buffalo: Christian Literature Publishing, 1890), revised and edited for New Advent by Kevin Knight, http://www.newadvent.org/fathers/26011.htm.

the good Shepherd, well known to those who study the sacred oracles, and that of Daniel also with the lions, forged in brass, and resplendent with plates of gold.[2]

We find, however, that Constantinople was also an outdoor museum of all the greatest art of the ancient pagan world. Eusebius tells us that Constantine pillaged statues of pagan gods from all over the empire and brought them to Constantinople.

On the other hand he used every means to rebuke the superstitious errors of the heathen. Hence the entrances of their temples in the several cities were left exposed to the weather, being stripped of their doors at his command; the tiling of others was removed, and their roofs destroyed. From others again the venerable statues of brass, of which the superstition of antiquity had boasted for a long series of years, were exposed to view in all the public places of the imperial city: so that here a Pythian, there a Sminthian Apollo, excited the contempt of the beholder; while the Delphic tripods were deposited in the circus, and the Muses of Helicon in the palace itself. In short, the city of Constantinople was everywhere filled with brazen statues of the most exquisite workmanship, which had been dedicated in every province, and which the deluded victims of superstition had long vainly honored as gods with numberless victims and burnt sacrifices, though now at length they learnt to renounce their error, when the emperor held up the very objects of their worship to be the ridicule and sport of all beholders.[3]

[2] Eusebius, *Life of Constantine* 3.48–49, trans. Ernest Cushing Richardson, in *NPNF*, 2nd series, vol. 1, ed. Philip Schaff and Henry Wace (Buffalo, N.Y.: Christian Literature Publishing, 1890), revised and edited for New Advent by Kevin Knight, http://www.newadvent.org/fathers/25023.htm.

[3] Ibid., 3.54.

By 330, the city was ready for the big transfer, and Constantine moved the seat of Roman government to Constantinople. Of course, the city had to have a bishop, and of course the bishop of Constantinople would be the bishop closest to the emperor. This was a great thing for an ambitious bishop. It was awful for a bishop who put faith and doctrine above ambition.

A Good Job for an Ambitious Bishop

Technically, the bishop of Constantinople was nobody special. For many years after Constantine, the city was the seat of an ordinary bishop, not an archbishop. But to a bishop who wanted influence, it was obviously the place to be.

In 339, just nine years after the capital moved to Constantinople, Eusebius of Nicomedia wrangled a transfer to Constantinople. In canon law it was a downgrade: Nicomedia was an important see, whereas Constantinople was still a suffragan see subject to the town of Heraclea. But Eusebius understood that being close to the emperor was better than having the canonical rank of archbishop. Standing beside Constantine, he could be the most important bishop in the world.

We've met Eusebius of Nicomedia before. He's the one who took up the cause of Arius in the Arian controversy—the cause that was apparently defeated when Constantine called the bishops together for the Council of Nicaea. It looked as though Eusebius had picked the losing side. But he was a slippery character, and he was determined to come out on top. He accepted the decision of Nicaea and then went to work convincing the emperor that his modified form of Arianism—Arianism Lite—was completely compatible with Nicene Christianity. If only Athanasius and those other fanatics weren't so stubborn, we could have peace! Somehow, by the end of Constantine's reign, it was Eusebius who was doing just fine, and the victors at Nicaea were having all the trouble. When Constantine was on his deathbed, he finally decided it was time to be baptized. (Many Christians delayed baptism until near death, supposing that it was better to wash away a lifetime's worth of sin at once.) And who would baptize him? Bishop Eusebius, of course.

Already politics in Constantinople was beginning to take on its characteristic form. In fact, the old name for the city has given us a name for that kind of politics: byzantine. It's the kind of politics where there are plots within plots and everybody is conspiring against everybody. Constantine himself had killed his own wife and son because he thought they were plotting against him.

After Constantine, it only got worse.

Byzantine Politics and the Man with the Golden Mouth

Constantine's son Constantius killed most of his near relatives, perhaps on the grounds that anybody related to him had to be up to no good. One of the few spared was a little boy named Julian, who grew up to be Julian the Apostate, the one whose beard was a running joke in Antioch. So maybe Constantius had the right instinct after all.

In 381, the First Council of Constantinople finally made official what had already been unofficially true: the see of Constantinople was second only to Rome in importance. That made the bishop's seat even more of a prize, and the politics around it even more byzantine.

In 397, the ancient bishop Nectarius died, and Arcadius the emperor wanted to find a replacement who would impress the people of Constantinople—possibly because Arcadius himself wasn't very impressive. Who better than that hotshot preacher who had been wowing the crowds in Antioch? John Chrysostom, the man who had preached the sermons about the statues, those sermons that had already become standard models for Christian rhetoricians, seemed like just the celebrity bishop for the imperial city.

Of course, Constantinople was a big prize, and there were plenty of people who had other opinions about who should be its bishop. One of them was Theophilus, bishop of Alexandria, who had a friend named Isidore who needed a job. Why not the Constantinople gig?

But John had an important booster in Constantinople. Eutropius the eunuch, who pretty much ran the empire under the weak-willed Arcadius, had decided John was the man for the job. Eutropius was an astute politician, which meant in those days that he had something to blackmail everybody with. There had been some complaints against Theophilus, and they would come up again if John wasn't ordained, Eutropius said. So Theophilus caved in and Isidore didn't get the job, which left Theophilus seething with resentment. And Theophilus was the kind of character who could keep a grudge going.

John, on the other hand, was not a politician. He was a great preacher, but when it came to playing the political games that were Theophilus' top skill, he just wasn't up to snuff. Worse yet, John would always go for the applause-getting line, even if he should have known it would get him in trouble.

Applause was a big thing in the Church in those days. When a preacher said something the congregation liked, they gave him enthusiastic applause. Sometimes John tried to persuade them to stop and listen in respectful silence, but when he said that they clapped and cheered. And he admitted he loved the applause. It made him feel good to know he had delivered a real zinger.

That would be his downfall.

The problem with the applause wasn't just that it stoked the preacher's vanity, or that it meant the congregation appreciated zingers more than sound doctrine. John saw that the love of applause could lead preachers to say things they shouldn't have said, merely for the sake of working the crowd.

If John had been as good at taking advice as he was at giving it, he might have had a much more comfortable life.

John Chrysostom had never really set out to be a celebrity preacher. What he had wanted to do with his life was to go out into the desert and live the life of an ascetic monk. But he was so rigorously ascetic that he ruined his health and had to come back to the city.

Nevertheless, he had an instinctive distaste for luxury, and he often preached sermons bashing the luxurious lives of the rich. The poor in his congregation cheered and clapped. Then he came to Constantinople—the seat of the emperor's court. If you hated luxury, Constantinople was not the place for you. The women of the court used *silver chamber pots*. John couldn't get over it. Is your excrement so important to you that you have to deposit it in silver?

You can imagine how the court ladies reacted to sermons like that. But we can be pretty sure the poor in the church were clapping and cheering. Who else gave them a sermon about chamber pots? Who else socked it to the rich like that? John was their hero. The applause kept coming.

Meanwhile, John lost his patron in a spectacular way. The usual conspiracies and counter-conspiracies finally caught up with Eutropius the eunuch, and he ended up fleeing to the Great Church (the cathedral) for refuge. There, while Eutropius was clinging to the altar, John preached a sermon on the text "All is vanity" from Ecclesiastes (1:2, 14). It was a masterpiece. He managed to persuade the emperor to let Eutropius leave the city safely and go into exile. Of course, the emperor brought him back a few months later to kill him, but that was byzantine politics for you.

John went back to offending the rich as usual, but now without the power of Eutropius to protect him from the consequences. Of all the offended court ladies, none was more implacably offended than the empress Eudoxia. John berated her for her greed and vanity. Vain and greedy empresses don't like that. She was determined to get rid of him. And who would help her do it? Well, the bishop of Alexandria was also nursing a grudge.

It took a lot of calling in favors and devious dealing, but Theophilus managed to have John condemned for heresy and exiled. Then strange things happened at the palace, and the superstitious emperor called him back. And what did John do? He insulted the empress *again*—this time over a statue of her that was the focus of public celebrations.

The next exile was his last. The emperor sent him farther and farther away, until John died at the far end of the Black Sea.

The Chrysostom affair established a precedent in Constantinople that would remain the rule for much of its history. When the patriarch and the emperor came into conflict, the emperor won. And it didn't matter that John's reputation was ultimately rehabilitated in Constantinople. He might be a saint, but his miserable earthly end was always there for the current patriarch of Constantinople to look back on.

This made the Church in the East diverge gradually from the Church in the West. When we come to Milan,

we'll meet a bishop who could tell one of the most powerful emperors in history that he had to wait outside with
the other repentant sinners until his bishop was good and
ready to let him back into church. Possibly by random
luck and possibly because of the characters of the bishops
involved, the precedent in the West was that the bishops
would not bow to the emperors' will. They might suffer
for it as much as John did, but the other bishops would
rally round, and the emperor would not get his way in
the end.

To a Catholic, moving the capital of the Roman Empire
away from Rome seems like part of the divine plan. It left
the popes in Rome hundreds of miles from the imperial
court. Even when the empire was divided into western
and eastern halves, the Western emperors usually lived at
either Milan or Ravenna; whole reigns could pass without an emperor setting foot in Rome. By 476, imperial
authority had almost completely vanished in the West.

Left to themselves, the popes could exercise an independent authority. They could base their decisions on
doctrine rather than on the whims of the imperial court.
And the Eastern bishops relied on that independence as
their only defense against the latest emperor's whims.

Maximus the Confessor

As for the emperors, they never learned. It was always an
irresistible temptation for Byzantine emperors to interfere
in theological controversies, and as the court became more
Byzantine, the sufferings of the bishops and theologians
who got in the emperor's way grew more extreme.

Maximus the Confessor was a monk and theologian who
happened to get caught up in a big fight over the question

of Jesus' will. The whole history of the age of the Fathers is a history of big fights over the nature of Christ. In this one, the question was whether Christ had only one will—a position known as *monothelitism*, from the Greek word meaning "one will". It seemed like a good compromise that might end the fight over whether Christ had two natures—a human nature and a divine nature—or only one. Emperors were supposed to bring people together, right?

But the theology was wrong. Rome weighed in: if Christ had a human and a divine nature, then Christ had a human and a divine will. This was not pleasing to the emperor. He ordered Maximus to fall in line. Maximus deferred to the decision of the pope. Now, Maximus never wanted to be a hero of the faith. He was just a peace-loving monk. He could be very accommodating. But the one thing he could not do was tell lies about the faith.

The emperor had his tongue cut out and his hand cut off, which was becoming the usual Byzantine style of discipline. Thus, Maximus earned his title of "confessor"—someone who suffered for the faith but was not an outright martyr.

Once again, Maximus was vindicated after he died. The Second Council of Constantinople—the sixth ecumenical council—decided he had been right about the double will of Christ. But the emperors never learned. They kept trying to force their own ideas of theology on the Church, and in the East they often succeeded.

The Eastern Roman Empire—historians call it the Byzantine Empire—somehow straggled on until 1453. For most of that time, Constantinople was its capital, although for a few decades in the 1200s, Constantinople fell into the hands of Western European Crusaders. By the 1400s, the city was pretty much all that was left of the Roman Empire, but it still took Mehmed the Conqueror a titanic effort to conquer it. The very last emperor was named Constantine—Constantine XI. He died fighting on the walls.

But the Turkish conquest didn't extinguish the Church in Constantinople. The patriarch of Constantinople is still the head of the Greek Orthodox Church. Until a century ago, Constantinople, or Istanbul to the Turks, still had a Greek population in the hundreds of thousands, but repeated outbreaks of ethnic violence chased most of the Greeks away, and today there are a few thousand at most.

10

Milan

Milan today is one of the most important cities in Europe. As a metropolitan center, it's bigger than Rome, and it's where you find the money in Italy if you're looking for rich people. It's the banking and industrial center of Italy and one of the fashion centers of the world.

In Christian history, though, Milan has a far more important place than money and fashion can give it. Milan was the place where the emperor Constantine and his partner (and soon to be enemy) Licinius issued the Edict of Milan, which made Christianity and all religions legal in the Roman Empire.

Mediolanum was the name of the city in ancient Roman times. But that's quite a mouthful, and the modern Italians have left out a few syllables. They call it *Milano*, the way natives of Baltimore call their city *Balmer*.

The Big Time

In the earlier days of the Roman Empire, Milan was an important regional city, but not one of the great urban centers. People from Rome itself probably thought of Milan the way New Yorkers think of Indianapolis. It was the capital of a province, and it had some well-known cultural institutions, but it wasn't anything Romans thought about very much.

But all that changed when the imperial capital moved from Rome to Milan.

To understand why that happened, we have to understand what a Roman emperor was. Today, when we hear "emperor", we think either of a figurehead, like the European royalty we see in clickbait gossip articles, or of a dictator with delusions of godhood. There were plenty of Roman emperors who were dictators with delusions of godhood, but the title *imperator* above all indicated a military leader. In fact, the founder of the institution, Augustus, wanted to be called *imperator* specifically because it had no connotations of royalty. He was a citizen doing his job, and his job just happened to be controlling the entire Roman Empire for the rest of his life.

For most of the history of the Roman Empire, the emperor was above all a military leader. His job was to see that the empire was defended from its enemies, and the ones who were remembered as *good* emperors led the soldiers into battle in person. In fact, the emperor was traditionally chosen by the soldiers; the Senate might confirm the choice, but the Senate had no choice itself.

Through much of the 200s, the Roman Empire was a mess, with emperors and would-be emperors fighting one another all over the place. Since emperors commonly gave the soldiers large gifts when they were chosen, the soldiers figured out that quick turnover was profitable. Not until the crusty soldier Diocletian was chosen emperor did the problems get sorted out.

Diocletian decided to reorganize everything, as we've heard before. For our story here, the most important change was that he divided the empire into two halves, each with its own emperor, and placed the Western emperor,

Maximian, in Milan rather than Rome. (Diocletian took the eastern half of the empire, making his capital at Nicomedia.) That way the emperor would be closer to the frontiers, where the action was. He would also be strategically placed to defend Italy and Rome from any land invasion, since Milan is right above the peninsula, in the plain that any barbarian army was likely to have to pass over to get to the rest of Italy.

Well, if Milan was going to be his imperial capital, Maximian was going to have to spiff it up a bit. He would need a palace, of course. Then he would need a circus to entertain the people and show them what a good emperor he was.

This was what happened to a city when the imperial court moved there, and of course all that money being spent attracted the top names in every profession. Milan became a boomtown, and soon it was rivaling Rome itself.

As far as the Church went, the bishop of Milan became a big deal. He was the one who would see the emperor in church every Sunday and hear the emperor's confessions. He was the one who was most likely to have a personal relationship with the emperor and have a chance to exercise some influence.

All this is why Milan was the scene of one of the most important events in Christian history—in fact, one of the most important events in history, period.

The Edict of Milan

As we remember, Diocletian's big plan for reforming the empire didn't work out too well. It ended with six emperors fighting one another all over the empire. One of them was Constantine, who, just before moving in on Rome, had a conversion experience and became a Christian.

That was in the year 312. The next year, he was in Milan, where his sister was marrying the junior partner in the empire, Licinius. A decade later, Constantine would execute his brother-in-law, but right now everything was jolly. The two emperors agreed on everything, and they issued a joint edict that said all people could choose their own religion.

> Among other matters we thought that nothing could be of greater advantage to our people, or concern ourselves more, than the settling of those matters in which the worship of the deity consisted; and therefore we judged it proper to allow to all Christians and others free liberty to follow that religion which they should like best: that by this means that supreme Deity who dwells on high might be gracious and favorable to us, and to all our subjects. Therefore upon due deliberation and weighty reasons, we have thought fit that no man may be denied the liberty of professing either the Christian religion or any other, as he shall judge it best; that so the great God, whom we worship with free minds, may in all things bless us with his gracious favor and protection.
>
> Therefore we will have you know that we have thought fit to annul all those restrictions that might seem to be in our former edict addressed to you relating to the Christians; and we do now ordain that everyone who is disposed to adhere to that religion shall be allowed to continue in it with all freedom, and without any disquiet or molestation. And we have explained this the more copiously to you, so that you might understand that we have given a free and absolute liberty to the said Christians to profess their religion.
>
> And since we have allowed this liberty to them, you will likewise understand that we allow the same free and

full liberty to all those who profess any other religion; so that, according to the quiet which we have brought the empire, every man may enjoy the free exercise of that religion of which he shall make choice for we will do nothing by which any man may suffer any prejudice either in his honor or on account of his religion.[1]

This was a turning point in the history of the world. For the first time in history, absolute tolerance of all religions was the law in a large part of the earth. It wouldn't last: Constantine's successors would crack down on the pagans and on the Christians they considered heretics. But the idea had been planted, and it is still here as an ideal today. No matter how far short of it we fall, we have the Edict of Milan to look up to.

Milan continued as the Western Roman capital for about a century. Because it was the residence of the emperor, Milan was more worked up over the Arian controversy than most of the West. Various members of the imperial family were Arians in the late 300s, and the Arian side was keen to establish itself as the legitimate church. The controversy was always on the verge of erupting into a riot.

All the work of sorting out the daily messes fell on the Roman governor of the province, Aurelius Ambrosius. We call him Ambrose in English. His job was to keep the two sides apart and try to satisfy them both—an impossible task, but Ambrose was so scrupulously fair that he earned the respect of both sides.

[1] Lactantius, *Deaths of the Persecutors* 48, in *God's Judgments upon Tyrants: Or a History of the Wicked Lives and Remarkable Deaths of Those Roman Emperors Who Persecuted the Primitive Christians. Written Originally in Latin by Lactantius. Made English by the Right Reverend Father in God Gilbert (Burnet) Lord Bishop of Sarum. By Whom Is Prefix'd, a Full View of Popery. In a Large Preface concerning Persecution*, 2nd ed. (London: Printed for J. Roberts near the Oxford Arms in Warwick Lane, 1715).

Ambrose for Bishop

The Arians had succeeded in getting one of their own installed as bishop of Milan, but when he died, both sides insisted that their candidate would be the new bishop. In those days, the bishop was chosen by the people, and when there was a controversy, that meant the people who shouted the loudest. Mobs from both sides were gathering in the Great Church (the cathedral). Some temperate soul ran off to tell the governor, "It looks like there's going to be a riot."

This was Governor Ambrose's constant nightmare. He ran to the church, where the two sides were already shouting at each other, and stood up to speak some calming words. Suddenly, a voice came from somewhere in the crowd: "Ambrose for bishop!" Ambrose tried to shrug it off and go on, but more and more voices—on both sides—took up the chant: "Ambrose for bishop! Ambrose for bishop!"

What could the poor governor do? He did what any sane man would do under the circumstances: he ran away and hid. It certainly was an awkward situation for Ambrose. Ambrose was a believer in the Christian faith, but he wasn't even baptized yet. (As we've already seen, many people delayed baptism until late in life.) He was a good governor, but nothing qualified him to be a bishop—or, at least, nothing but his natural disposition and talents.

An obliging friend let Ambrose hide out at his house for a while. But then a letter came from the emperor himself (who was away on imperial business at the time) congratulating the people of Milan on such a wise choice of bishop. The friend decided it was a done deal and turned Ambrose over to his fate. In one week, he was baptized, ordained, and consecrated bishop.

Now we see why Ambrose was so keen to avoid this dubious honor. Other people might think it was just a job. Not Ambrose. He really was a believer. If he was going to be bishop, he would have to do it right. He sold everything he had—and he was rich—and distributed it to the poor. He held back just enough to keep his sister Marcellina, a consecrated virgin, modestly comfortable.

This convinced the people of Milan that they had made the right choice. They were sure they had picked a man "known to the whole world as among the best of men", as Saint Augustine would later say of him.[2]

Ambrose settled in for a crash course in Christian theology. With his giant brain, he mastered the subject. Augustine would later remember that he read silently, which was unheard of: the usual practice was to read a book out loud. Augustine guessed it was the only way Ambrose could get any reading done without people interrupting him and asking him to explain what he was reading, since he was always surrounded by people and never turned away visitors.

Ambrose was a riveting preacher who could make the truths of Christian theology both interesting and understandable to the people who filled his church. He was also known for his kindness to everyone. There was only one group who were not pleased with him. The Arians had thought he would continue to steer an impartial middle course between the Arians and the Orthodox Catholics. They were wrong. That was Ambrose the governor, whose job was to keep the peace. Now they were dealing with Ambrose the bishop, whose job was to shepherd

[2] Augustine, *Confessions* 5.13.23, trans. J. G. Pilkington, in *NPNF*, 1st series, vol. 1, ed. Philip Schaff (Buffalo, N.Y.: Christian Literature Publishing, 1887), revised and edited for New Advent by Kevin Knight, http://www.newadvent.org/fathers/110105.htm.

the Christian flock of Milan. He became the implacable enemy of Arianism—always kind to individuals but never wavering in his insistence on Catholic truth.

This was the Ambrose who started Saint Augustine down the path to conversion. He did it not by badgering him or arguing with him but by showing him that intelligent people could be Christian and could have good reasons for it. Above all, he did it by being a friend.

This was also the Ambrose who faced down the emperor Theodosius.

Making the Emperor See Reason

We talked about Theodosius right at the beginning of our trip through these twelve ancient cities. He was the terrifying example of what could happen to a whole city if there was a riot that displeased the emperor. In Thessalonica, there had been a riot. It started with sports hooligans. The races were the most popular form of entertainment, and when a popular charioteer was arrested (for a crime of which he was probably guilty), the fans erupted. They ended up killing a Roman official.

When Theodosius heard about it, he was furious. He was a notorious hothead. As Ambrose himself would tell him, "You have a natural ferociousness. If anyone tries to soothe it, you quickly turn to mercy. If any one stirs it up, you rouse it so much more that you can scarcely restrain it."[3] In his first fury, he sent orders for a general indiscriminate

[3] Ambrose, *Letter* 51.4, trans. H. de Romestin, E. de Romestin, and H. T. F. Duckworth, in *NPNF*, 2nd series, vol. 10, ed. Philip Schaff and Henry Wace (Buffalo, N.Y.: Christian Literature Publishing, 1896), revised and edited for New Advent by Kevin Knight, http://www.newadvent.org/fathers/340951.htm.

massacre of the citizens of Thessalonica. Shortly after that, he realized what a horrible thing he had done, and he sent orders to countermand the first order. But it was too late. Thousands died, most of them innocent.

This put Ambrose in a very difficult situation. Everyone heard about the massacre, and Ambrose, as bishop of Milan, was the man responsible for the Church's relations with the emperor. He was Theodosius' confessor. What should he do? He had seen what happened when Theodosius had a tantrum. It would have been easiest just to shrug and say that emperors will be emperors.

But that was not what Ambrose chose. The emperor had committed a mortal sin. He was excommunicated until he had done proper penance. And it would have to be penance everyone could see so that his example would show that even the emperor was not above God's law.

Ambrose explained his reasons in a long and carefully worded letter to the emperor. He was courteous and kind, but he was explicit. He could not just dismiss what Theodosius had done.

> What was done in the city of the Thessalonians was something of which no similar record exists. I was not able to prevent it from happening. Indeed, I had said before that it would be a terrible atrocity. I begged you over and over not to do it, and by revoking it too late you show that you yourself consider it to be grave.
>
> I could not extenuate it when you had done it. When the news first came in, a synod had met because of the arrival of the Gallican Bishops. There was not one who did not lament it, not one who thought lightly of it; the fact that you were in fellowship with Ambrose was no excuse for your deed. Everyone would have piled the blame for it on me if no one had said that it was necessary for you to be reconciled to God.

Are you ashamed, Emperor, to do what the royal prophet David did—David the forefather of Christ according to the flesh? He was told how the rich man who had many flocks seized and killed the poor man's one lamb, because of the arrival of his guest, and recognizing that he himself was being condemned in the tale—for he himself had done it—he said, "I have sinned against the Lord."[4] Bear it, then, without impatience, O Emperor, if you are told, "You have done that which was spoken of to King David by the prophet." For if you listen obediently to this, and say: "I have sinned against the Lord," if you repeat those words of the royal prophet: "O come, let us worship and bow down, let us kneel before the Lord, our Maker!" (Psalm 95:6), it shall be said to you also, since you repent, "The Lord also has put away your sin; you shall not die" (2 Samuel 12:13)....

I have written this, not in order to confound you, but that the examples of these kings may stir you up to put away this sin from your kingdom, for you will do it away by humbling your soul before God. You are a man, and it has come upon you. Conquer it. Sin is only done away by tears and penitence. Neither angel can do it, nor archangel. The Lord himself, who alone can say, "I am with you" (Matthew 28:20), does not forgive us if we have sinned unless we repent.

I urge, I beg, I exhort, I warn, for it is a grief to me, that you who were an example of unusual piety, who were conspicuous for clemency, who would not suffer single offenders to be put in peril, should not mourn that so many have perished. Though you have waged battle most successfully, though in other matters, too, you are worthy of praise, yet piety was always the crown of your actions. The devil envied your most excellent possession. Conquer

---

[4] Ambrose is referring to the incident of Bathsheba's husband, whom David sent to be killed in battle so that he could have Bathsheba for himself. See 2 Samuel 11–12.

him while you still possess the means to conquer. Do not
add another sin to your sin by a course of action that has
injured many.[5]

The legacy of Saint Ambrose in the Western Church
is incalculable. He was a great theologian who left us
powerful dogmatic writings. He was also a great poet
who began a tradition of singable hymns in popular language. The Archdiocese of Milan still has its own particular form of the Catholic liturgy called the Ambrosian
Rite, which preserves some different traditions from the
usual Roman Rite.

But the most important legacy of Ambrose is an
assumption that has pervaded the Western Church. When
the Church and the government come into conflict, the
Church will not bend. We could hardly say the Church
has always been faithful to this principle; individual bishops have certainly bent at various times. But the Western
Catholic Church has always come back to it. When it is
a matter of Christian truth, the truth comes before the
emperor—even if the emperor is a hothead.

As for Milan itself, it had its ups and downs through
the rest of history. Not long after the time of Ambrose, it
ceased to be the imperial capital, which is why our next
stop will be Ravenna, the city that took Milan's place as
home of the emperor. During the Byzantine reconquest
of Italy, Milan was nearly destroyed, although a basilica
founded by Saint Ambrose still stands today. After that, the
archbishops of Milan became the main secular authorities
as well as the leaders of the Church there. But Roman
imperial history moves to Ravenna.

---

[5] Ambrose, *Letter* 51.6–7, 11–12.

Ravenna

The sea is what makes Ravenna such a valuable place. It has always been a settlement, but it grew into an important city when the emperor Augustus, with his sharp military mind, saw that it was the perfect place to station a Roman fleet. On every side, the location was surrounded by impassable swamps, so land enemies could never sneak up on the place. Canals gave it access to the sea and to the valley of the river Po, from which friendly forces could easily supply the fleet. And from there the fleet could control the whole Adriatic.

The town that rapidly grew around the base was called Classis—Latin for "fleet". Soon another and larger town grew nearby on a patch of dry land big enough for a city in the otherwise inhospitable muck of the coastal marshes. This was what became Ravenna. Even today Ravenna is still separated from Classe, the modern name for Classis, by a short stretch of empty road through the flats.

Ravenna was a fairly big city, but it remained a city of secondary importance for the first four centuries of the Christian era. Rome was the imperial capital at first, and other Italian cities were bigger and more important than Ravenna. As barbarian invasions began to be regular problems, the emperors used Milan as their base to be closer to the barbarian incursions and to be able to defend the Italian peninsula from attack from the north.

A Perfect Place for a Coward

The story of Ravenna as capital begins with Theodosius the Great. We've met him before—he was the hothead who nearly destroyed Antioch but also the military genius who held the empire together. No one knew it at the time, but he would be the last Roman emperor to rule over both the Eastern Empire and the Western.

Theodosius had three children who survived to adult-hood: brothers Arcadius and Honorius and their half sister, Galla Placidia, born to Theodosius' second wife after his first wife died. He also adopted his orphaned niece Serena, who was older than any of his biological children. Serena married the very successful general Stilicho, who would end up being more or less the founder of Ravenna as an imperial capital.

It was Theodosius who really made the Roman Empire Christian. Since Constantine, the emperors had all been Christians except for the short-reigned Julian the Apostate, but they had allowed the pagan cults to go on with public support, especially in the city of Rome, where the con-servative aristocracy remained mostly pagan. Theodosius put a stop to that: he cut off the public funds for pagan celebrations. Since the Roman Senate could not imagine any other way of funding them, that effectively brought an end to them.

Like several of the emperors before him, Theodosius made Milan his capital when he was in the West. He died there in 395 at the age of forty-eight, leaving his two sons in charge of the empire. The problem with that was that his sons were still very young. Arcadius, who was in charge of the East, was seventeen. Honorius, the new Western emperor, was ten.

Obviously, the boys were going to need some help. Fortunately, Theodosius had provided each of them with a talented general to do the heavy lifting in the imperial government. In the East, Rufinus would guide Arcadius; in the West, Stilicho would take care of things while Honorius grew a little older.

Stilicho was an ambitious man, and while Honorius was a child, it was really Stilicho who was in charge. There's no good evidence that he plotted to gain the imperial throne for himself, but he certainly wouldn't mind if one of his children or grandchildren got it. He arranged to have his daughter, who was twelve, marry Honorius when he was thirteen.

Honorius' long childhood set up a new pattern for the Roman emperor of the West. Instead of being a military leader like his father, Theodosius, who expected to run toward the trouble wherever it broke out, Honorius was a valuable asset to be protected by Stilicho and kept as far away from danger as possible.

When Gothic invaders started menacing Italy, Stilicho decided the imperial capital at Milan was too exposed. It had been chosen because it was close to the action. Now being close to the action was the problem. Stilicho recommended Ravenna as a safe place for Honorius to keep out of trouble while his generals took care of everything. It was as far away from the barbarians as he could get. The qualities that made it such an admirable base for the fleet also made it the perfect capital for an emperor who was a complete coward. The city was surrounded by vast acreage of swamps and marshes, which effectively served as a defensive moat. Any army that attempted an approach would soon find itself bogged and at least delayed. So in 402, the emperor Honorius declared Ravenna the new administrative capital of the Western Empire.

At the end of the fourth century, Ravenna's population hovered around fifty thousand—a big city, certainly, but not a first-class city. Now, as a capital, it would experience a full flourishing of culture. With the emperor came the court, and with the court came an abundance of treasure. Ravenna now became the destination for the Western Empire's best and brightest—in rhetoric, in the sciences, and in the arts.

Barbarian Troubles

Meanwhile, the rest of the empire was falling to pieces. Stilicho defeated one invader after another, but then his enemies persuaded Honorius that Stilicho was plotting against him. Stilicho and all his associates were executed— even Honorius' adopted sister, Serena.

That left Honorius without an effective general who could keep the invaders at bay. The Goths were the most formidable. Their leader, Alaric, wanted to replace Stilicho as top Roman general, and if Honorius had agreed to the terms his subordinates negotiated with Alaric, he might have had the formidable Gothic armies on his side instead of as his enemies. But Honorius had a genius for making enemies. Finally, Alaric besieged Rome. Honorius didn't seem to care much. He was safe in Ravenna, where he enjoyed his hobby of keeping fancy poultry.

His half sister, Galla Placidia, however, was stuck in Rome. She seems to have made a dramatic attempt to slip through the besieging Goths and escape from the city—but she failed. She was captured and held as a bargaining chip.

Finally, the Goths broke through to Rome in 410, as we already heard when we visited Rome. They plundered whatever they could carry, but they allowed citizens—including many pagans—to take refuge in the great churches, where Alaric ordered his soldiers to leave them alone. Honorius sat in Ravenna and played with his fancy chickens.

Alaric died of disease in southern Italy shortly after carrying away the loot from Rome. His successor, Athaulf, married the Roman hostage Galla Placidia—the emperor's own half sister. Was it against her will? Probably not. She may have sized up her brother pretty well and decided he would never amount to anything as Roman emperor. She and her new Gothic husband seem to have meant to found a new imperial family that would combine the Gothic and the Roman in one unstoppable force. They had a son named Theodosius, after Galla Placidia's father, the great emperor. But the boy died young, and shortly afterward, Athaulf was murdered by one of his own subordinates.

The widowed Galla Placidia was soon sent back to Ravenna in exchange for supplies the Goths desperately needed. There Honorius arranged for her to marry Constantius, the general who had replaced Stilicho. They had a daughter named Honoria and a son named Valentinian. Shortly afterward, Constantius was made co-emperor, with Galla Placidia taking the role of *Augusta* and little Valentinian becoming *Nobilissimus*, presumably on his way to being emperor someday. But Constantius died just a few months after becoming emperor, and Galla Placidia was a widow once more. After rumors that Honorius had fallen in love with his own half sister, Galla Placidia was sent to Constantinople.

Eventually, Honorius fizzled out at the age of thirty-eight, like a flickering candle drowning in its own wax. After his death, one of his bureaucrats tried to make himself emperor, but Galla Placidia came back to Ravenna with a strong force from Constantinople, and the usurper was defeated and killed. That left Valentinian as undisputed emperor of the West. Since he was only six years old, though, he would need someone to do the actual ruling. And his mom was up to the task.

Galla Placidia and Peter Chrysologus

This is how Galla Placidia came to be ruler of the Western Empire, a role she seemed to relish. For the story of Ravenna, it was tremendously important, because Placidia was a devout Catholic Christian, and she began filling the city with beautiful churches. She made a close alliance with the new bishop of Ravenna, Peter, known as Chrysologus—"Golden Speech"—for his eloquent sermons.

One of the things people loved about his homilies was that they were *short*. Peter kept them that way deliberately. He thought people would stop paying attention if he rambled on too long. Occasionally, Peter even ended his sermons abruptly, explaining that it was his custom not to weary his congregations.

Well, there's a lot to be said for a short homily. And a lot can be said *in* a short homily. Maybe some podcasters could learn a few tricks from Peter.

Short homilies, in fact, are pretty much all we have from Peter Chrysologus. They're almost all we know with certainty about him. But based entirely on his corpus of short homilies, he is revered today as a Father of the Church, as a saint, and as a Doctor of the Church. He's even called the Doctor of Homilies.

Born in Imola, Italy, in the last years of the fourth century, Peter was a disciple of the bishop there, whose name was Cornelius. Cornelius baptized him, educated him, and ordained him a deacon. We know nothing about his accomplishments in those years, but he must have made an impression in the Church in Italy, because around the year 426, the pope in Rome chose Peter of Imola for a very important assignment. He named him bishop of the city of Ravenna.

But first a word about his name. In his lifetime, he was Peter of Imola. Not till the ninth century do we find evidence of the nickname Chrysologus. It appears in a biography larded with legend by an abbot named Andrew Agnellus, who tells us Peter received the title from the regent empress after he preached his inaugural homily in the city. She declared him to be "Peter of the golden words"—Peter Chrysologus.

What is more likely is that the West wanted its own golden preacher, since the East had Saint John Chrysostom. So Peter posthumously received the title and the legend to go with it.

It is true, however, that Peter arrived in Ravenna eagerly awaited by the empress and the court, and his first task was to preach to them. He preached to her on his opening day, and he preached to her on many Sundays and holy days afterward. They became famous as co-workers, building the churches that have made Ravenna a tourist destination. But they also competed with one another in acts of piety. A contemporary historian in Gaul describes their figurative tug-of-war over the relics of a recently deceased holy man. In the end, Galla Placidia kept the saint's body for the empire, and Peter received his clothing and hair shirt for the Church.

Placidia and Peter shared several basic religious principles. They held to Nicene orthodoxy as it was confirmed and developed at the Council of Constantinople and later at Ephesus. And they were fiercely and traditionally Roman in their sense of papal authority.

In fact, the only letter of Peter's that has survived is his response to an appeal he had received from the heretic Eutyches. He refuses to make judgment, because he insists that the word of Pope Leo the Great must be the final word. He tells Eutyches, "However, we give you this exhortation in regard to everything, honorable brother: obediently heed those matters in which the most blessed Pope of the City of Rome has written, because

blessed Peter who lives and presides in his own see prof-
fers the truth of faith to those who seek it."[1] That letter
survives because a copy somehow made its way to Rome
and was filed away with Pope Leo's correspondence.
Otherwise, what we know of Peter's "golden words" are
his sermons.

Over the course of his sermons, he also makes a lively
response to the heresies of his time—all of which must
have made their presence known in the capital city. He
shows special concern for Arianism, because it was the religion of many of the barbarian mercenaries in the Roman
military. But he also saw lingering effects of Nestorianism,
which had only recently been condemned by the Council
of Ephesus. In short, he was concerned about the matters
that really affected his people. And he treated them with
clarity, concision, and brevity. But the greatest of these
was brevity.

While Peter was bishop, Ravenna was elevated to a
metropolitan see—and so he became an archbishop.

He may be the only Church Father you can see today
in a portrait produced during his lifetime. It's in Ravenna's
Church of Saint John the Evangelist, which Galla Placidia
built in thanksgiving after she had a brush with death at
sea. There, in the apse, is a mosaic depicting Peter as he
offers Mass on a ship. So perhaps he shared that perilous
voyage. He has white hair, a long beard, and wide eyes.
His friend Galla Placidia is standing there with him.

In 450, Peter undertook a journey to his hometown of
Imola. We don't know why. But we know he died there.
Galla Placidia died that same year.

---

[1] Saint Peter Chrysologus, *Letter to Eutyches*, in *Saint Peter Chrysologus: Selected Sermons; and Saint Valerian: Homilies*, trans. George E. Ganss, S.J. (New York: Fathers of the Church, 1953), p. 286.

A quarter century later, the last Western emperor would turn in his papers and the barbarian king Odoacer would rule in Italy.

Not Much Happens in Ravenna

It was the end of the Western Roman Empire, but it wasn't the end of Ravenna's glory. In fact, under the Gothic king Theodoric, who replaced Odoacer (by murdering him), Ravenna flourished. It almost seemed like a new golden age for Italy.

Then came a very dark age, when the successors of Theodoric battled a new invasion, this time by the Romans. Justinian, the emperor in Constantinople, had decided he would reconquer the Western Empire. His brilliant general, Belisarius, succeeded in taking back Italy—but only after years of war that left the whole peninsula devastated.

Ravenna was spared most of the damage, however, and under Justinian the city flourished. You can see his picture in the Basilica of San Vitale, rendered in stunning mosaic, along with the empress Theodora and the whole court. They were never actually in Ravenna, but those portraits, as identifiable as passport photos, represented their symbolic presence in the capital of the Roman West.

After Justinian, most of Italy was reconquered by Westerners again. A strip across the middle, including Rome and Ravenna, remained part of the Eastern Roman Empire for two more centuries. It was Ravenna that was the capital of the Exarchate of Italy, where the representatives of Constantinople made their devious byzantine deals with their neighbors and preserved a sliver of Roman power in what had once been the imperial heartland.

The extraordinary thing about Ravenna since classical times is that it has been a place where not much happened. Because not much happened, the remains of its days as an imperial capital, as well as its time during Theodoric's reign and the Byzantine reconquest, are still there for us to see. The city didn't prosper the way Florence or Venice did, so most of its ancient monuments weren't replaced with bigger and grander ones in later ages. But they never decayed enough for them to fall into ruin.

Today the early Christian art and architecture of Ravenna—and above all its glorious mosaics—are one of the world's great treasures, a UNESCO World Heritage site. It's one of the few places on earth where you can walk into a church and have almost the same experience one of the Fathers of the Church would have had.

12

Carthage

Carthago delenda est. "Also, Carthage must be destroyed."

That was how the famously inflexible senator Cato ended every speech in the Roman Senate for years. That's how Carthage enters Roman history, and that's how our histories remember it today: as the enemy of Rome that must be defeated at any cost. After a century of war on and off, it finally *was* defeated in 146 B.C., nearly a century and a half before the birth of Christ. The Romans leveled the city, sold tens of thousands of survivors into slavery, and destroyed the power of Carthage forever.

If that were the end of the story, we wouldn't be talking about Carthage right now.

But a new story began a hundred years later, when Rome rebuilt Carthage on a rational Roman plan. That was the city of Carthage that would go on to be one of the great centers of Christian culture in the ancient world. In fact, this African city and its surroundings are at the root of Western Christian culture.

People are surprised to hear that. Isn't Rome at the root of Western Christian culture? Why would you say Carthage—a city most people these days have never even heard of?

To understand what Carthage was like and why it was so important to the Christian West, we have to understand its complicated and confusing history.

The Tumultuous History of Northern Africa

In the beginning, there were Berbers. No matter how many waves of immigrants have washed across North Africa, the Berbers have always remained.

About eight hundred years before Christ, colonists from Tyre arrived at Carthage and started to build a city. Tyre was the most famous of all the great Phoenician cities that sent sailing ships trading throughout the Mediterranean. "Tyre, who dwells at the entrance to the sea, merchant of the peoples on many islands"—that was what the prophet Ezekiel called the place (Ezek 27:3). From Tyre, the people of Carthage brought their language, their sailing skill, and their eye for a good deal. Punic—the language of the Phoenicians— became the language of the city of Carthage and the ruling class in the surrounding area. Tyre itself was conquered by the Assyrians. Ezekiel sang a dirge for the city: "Who was ever destroyed like Tyre in the midst of the sea?" (27:32).

That left Carthage to go its own way—and Carthage flourished. It grew to be one of the biggest cities in the world, controlling a mighty empire that stretched from the edge of Egypt to the shores of the Atlantic, and across the Mediterranean to Spain, Sardinia, Corsica, and Sicily. But that brought it into conflict with the other expanding empire in the western Mediterranean, and we know how that ended up. After a century of conflict, Rome conquered and destroyed Carthage and made the territory around the city the Roman province of Africa.

Now the language of the ruling class was Latin. But the Punic-speaking population was still there, and so was the Berber-speaking population. People would still be speaking Punic for hundreds of years after the conquest of Carthage. Millions of people still speak Berber today.

After a century of leaving the site deserted, the Romans decided the harbor of Carthage was too good to go to waste. They laid out a new city according to the latest theories of rational urban planning, and Carthage began to grow at once. By about two hundred years after Christ, it was the second-largest Latin-speaking city in the world. Only Rome was bigger.

Africa was the breadbasket of Rome: the poorest citizens in the capital ate bread made from African grain. All the riches of Africa were shipped through Carthage, which made the city richer and richer.

All those people traveling to and from Carthage must have brought Christianity very early. We have no records of the beginnings of the Church in Roman Africa. When we first hear of it, it's already everywhere.

The Scillitan Martyrs

The Church first bursts into history in the case of the Scillitan Martyrs, twelve people who were executed for Christianity in the year 180. Because the Roman government kept records of everything, the way bureaucracies love to do, the transcript of their trial was available for Christians to copy. It shows that this trial went the way most of these trials did: the judge tried to persuade the Christians to take the *reasonable* way out and just offer a pagan sacrifice and go on with their lives, and the Christians said they were very sorry but they couldn't do that.

These twelve people came from a little town called Scillium in the backcountry of Africa. If there were Christians way out in the boondocks, there must have been thousands of them already in Carthage. It was the commercial hub and one of the great trading cities of the world. Everything that came to Africa came to Carthage first.

But it wasn't just commerce that made Carthage one of the great cities of the Roman Empire. North Africa also grew into one of the great centers of Latin literary culture. Some of the greatest names in Latin literature came from the province of Africa. Terence, who wrote comedies that still make us laugh today, is the earliest Latin writer whose work has come down to us in a substantial body—and his name, Publius Terentius Afer, probably tells us he came from Africa. Apuleius wrote a novel called *The Golden Ass* about a man who gets changed into a donkey, and it's the only Latin novel from ancient times that has survived in its entirety. Suetonius, the historian of the early emperors, and Fronto, who codified the principles of Latin rhetoric, were Africans.

And then there was Tertullian.

The Founder of Latin Christian Literature

It comes as a surprise to most people that the first important Christian writer in Latin was from Africa, not Rome. But the Christian Church in Rome spoke Greek for the first couple of hundred years. Its liturgy was in Greek, and its writers set their thoughts down in Greek. That's probably because Rome had a huge Greek-speaking population among the merchants and craftsmen—just the demographic where Christianity took hold and grew fastest.

Africa was different. From a very early age, its liturgy was in Latin. Our Latin Mass began in Africa, not in Rome. *All* the important Latin Christian writers of the first three centuries are associated with Africa.

Tertullian came from Carthage. He was born about 155, and he was converted to Christianity early in his life. He also had the best education Carthage had to offer. When he became a Christian, he applied all that education to writing about his new faith.

Christian writing might be very different now without Tertullian. The faith would be the same, but our ways of explaining it wouldn't have so many perfect terms that he came up with. "Trinity", for one—Tertullian invented that word to explain what Christians believed about one God in three Persons.

He also set a standard for Christian literature that would make it different from the pagan Latin literature Africa was known for. Writers like Apuleius delighted in their sophistication. They picked out the biggest and most obscure words they could find just to show off. But Tertullian wrote directly in the Latin of ordinary people. He put the most exalted Christian theology in terms anybody could understand.

Late in life, Tertullian veered off into a schismatic group, the Montanists, who believed that the majority Church was too lenient with Christians who had renounced their faith during the persecutions and now wanted to return to the Church. But his writings were too valuable to give up. Even though he was a schismatic, the next great Christian writer from Africa always referred to Tertullian as "the Master".

Cyprian and the Question of the Lapsed

That next great writer was Cyprian, the bishop of Carthage. He disagreed with Tertullian fundamentally on exactly the issue that made Tertullian join the Montanists.

Saint Cyprian became bishop in 249, and shortly after that, Decius became emperor. Decius was the kind of emperor who was going to fix everything that was wrong with the world. Looking around him, he discovered that one of the main things wrong with the world was that it had Christians in it. They refused to sacrifice to the gods who had made Rome great!

So Decius decided to fix that.

Until the time of Decius, persecutions had been local, and most Christians lived peaceful lives most of the time. But Decius decided that all citizens would have to *prove* they weren't Christian by making a public sacrifice to the pagan gods. In proper bureaucratic fashion, the *good* citizens who sacrificed would receive a certificate, which they would have to present on demand. The ones who refused would die.

With the whole machinery of Roman government bearing down on them, and all the most creative Roman tortures lined up to persuade them, many Christians gave up and got their certificates. When the persecution slowed down, some of those people felt the guilt of what they had done and wanted to come back into the Church.

What should be done about that? Some said they could never come back. God *might* forgive them, but the Church couldn't. Some extremists believed there was no forgiveness for *any* serious sin committed after baptism. Others said they would take them back, no questions asked. Cyprian steered the middle course—the right course. A period of penitence would be required. The lapsed would have to show they were really sincere about repenting. But if they kept it up, they could come back into communion.

Saint Cyprian avoided martyrdom during the persecution of Decius by leaving the city. Some Christians thought he should have gone cheerfully to death, but once again he advocated a middle course—escape if you can, but if you're backed into a corner and face the choice of renouncing Christ or dying, then you die. Under the next emperor, Valerian, Cyprian was backed into that corner. Without the least hesitation, he died.

Cyprian didn't settle the question of the lapsed. A whole alternative church grew up around the Christians who refused to forgive the people who had broken under the persecutions. They would end up rallying around a man named Donatus, and the Donatists would continue to be a problem for more than a century. In time, they coalesced with various groups who were discontented with the Roman government and became a kind of terrorist movement, attacking governors and orthodox bishops. We've almost forgotten about them today, but in their time, they made so much trouble that they took up much of the mental effort of the greatest Christian writer who came out of Roman Africa, Saint Augustine.

Augustine, Proud to Be African

We know more about Augustine than we know about any other North African Christian. In fact, we probably know more about Augustine than we know about any other person from the ancient world. Not only did he leave us a whole shelf of great books, but he also wrote the first autobiography in the modern sense—the *Confessions*. If you haven't read that book yet, you need to read it. It's probably the most popular Christian book outside the Bible itself, and it's popular for good reason. Other writers, like Julius Caesar, had set down histories of their glorious deeds. But Augustine was the first to tear open his own soul on the page and examine everything in it.

Augustine was born in 354 in a little town called Tagaste. His mother was Christian, but his father was pagan. Augustine's father sacrificed a lot of comforts so that his son could have the best education available, and it paid off. As a young man, Augustine moved to the big city—Carthage—and became one of the most sought-after teachers of rhetoric there.

Carthage presented all kinds of temptations to a young man. Augustine took up a mistress there—that was one of the big-city temptations. But Carthage also had its intellectual temptations, and Augustine joined the Manicheans, a dualistic cult that took a little from this religion and a little from that and put them all together in a way that appealed to young intellectuals like Augustine.

Meanwhile, his mother prayed constantly for Augustine's conversion. We remember her today as Saint Monica. Everybody's mother is a saint, of course, but Monica put more effort into it than most.

Augustine was a standout teacher in Carthage, and he figured there would be even more opportunities if he went to Rome. He was right. Once he was in Rome, the prefect of the city—a pagan, like a lot of the upper class in Rome—noticed his talents and recommended him to the emperor in Milan. So Augustine got a plum job in Milan. And that was the best thing that ever happened to him, because in Milan he met Saint Ambrose.

Augustine had already been losing patience with the Manicheans. When difficult questions came up, he couldn't find any Manichean who could answer them. But Ambrose was different. At first, Augustine went to hear his sermons because everyone said they were great entertainment— and they were. But Ambrose also had answers. He made *sense*. Augustine, the snobby young intellectual, had always thought of Christianity as the faith of the poor and ignorant. Yet here was one of the great brains of the age explaining the Christian faith and answering all the questions the Manicheans couldn't touch.

That opened Augustine's mind. After all those years of his mother praying for him, one day Augustine picked up the Scriptures, read a few lines, and found himself a Christian. Once he was a Christian, all of Augustine's prodigious talent went into writing about his faith. He wrote and wrote. The *Catechism of the Catholic Church* cites him more often than any other writer outside those in the Bible.

He went back to Africa, where he became bishop of Hippo, a fairly substantial city near Carthage. He spent the rest of his life there, and he was always proud to tell people he was an African, one who had grown up hearing the Punic language and could still speak some of it, though Latin was his native tongue.

When the Goths sacked Rome in 410, it sent ripples of horror throughout the empire. The remaining pagans put on their told-you-so faces and blamed the Christians for neglecting the ancient gods who had made Rome great. Augustine responded by writing his biggest book, the only one that competes with the *Confessions* in its influence: *The City of God*. He explained that Christians suffer the same calamities on this earth that everyone else does. But Christians belong to the city of God, not the city of this world.

It was good for Augustine to have the consolation of knowing that disasters didn't mean God had forsaken his people. He lived to see the end of Roman Africa approaching. In 430, as the Germanic Vandals were besieging Hippo, Augustine died. The Vandals would go on to conquer all of Roman Africa and rule it for a hundred years, adding a Germanic layer to the multiple layers of languages and cultures there.

These Vandals were also Christians, but they were Arian Christians—and extremely bigoted ones. The Catholic majority found themselves persecuted as brutally as they had been in pagan times. The persecution came to an end only when Justinian's armies reconquered Africa for the Eastern Roman Empire.

This wasn't as much of an improvement as the Orthodox Africans had hoped it would be. Everything was ruled from Constantinople, and Constantinople expected that the Western Christians would conform to Eastern practice. But what made Latin Christianity distinctive was, above all, that it was African. For a century and a half, Carthage found itself aligned with the pope and the rest of the West against the governing powers in the East. Then came the Arab conquest, and African Christianity gradually faded.

But that's not really true. African Christianity is still very much with us. Wherever a church is celebrating Mass according to the Latin Rite, that's African Christianity. Wherever a theologian is arguing a point by citing Saint Augustine, that's African Christianity. Wherever a Christian is appealing to the Trinity, that's African Christianity. The Christian tradition of Roman Africa, the ancient faith of Carthage, is invisible not because it has disappeared but because it has become the very air we breathe.

AFTERWORD

The Lessons of the Cities

We've visited some famous cities and a few you'd probably never heard of before you opened this book. They were all different, but they all had things in common as well.

The biggest similarity is that they were all shaped by the Roman Empire. Most of them were in the Roman Empire, at least for most of the period of history we were talking about. But even the ones that were outside the Roman Empire weren't outside Roman influence. Many of the Fathers of the Church believed that the Roman Empire had a providential purpose, unifying the known world so that the Gospel could spread unhindered. We've seen how the open conditions of the Roman Empire, the lack of borders and the extensive trade with faraway places, made it possible for the faith to spread rapidly from one city to the next.

Jerusalem was where the Christian faith began. It had been the center of the faith of Israel since King David's time, and it was where every faithful Jew who could get there went to make sacrifices at the Temple. It was where Jesus collided with the Temple authorities, and it was where those authorities thought they had won their final victory over him by persuading the Roman governor to sentence him to death. But Jerusalem would turn out to be the place where Jesus won the final victory over death itself.

189

That makes Jerusalem the most important city in Christian history.

Yet Christianity can get along without Jerusalem. For most of history, it *has* got along without Jerusalem. Today there are Christians in the city, but they're a minority. For centuries, Jerusalem was ruled by Muslim empires. Now it is ruled by a secular Jewish state. The Catholic Church grew to be the largest religious organization on the planet without Jerusalem. That's an important lesson to remember.

Through the Middle Ages, most Western European Christians drew their maps of the world with Jerusalem at the center. Yet most Western European Christians never saw Jerusalem. Jerusalem was at the center of their thought as Christians, because Christianity is historical. The fundamental truth of Christian faith is that God came to us in a particular place, at a particular time, as a particular Person.

It's a very good thing to make a pilgrimage to Jerusalem to see the holy places. I've done it. It puts your mind in touch with the reality of Jesus' life, death, and Resurrection. But a pilgrimage to Jerusalem isn't *necessary* for your Christian faith. If Jerusalem vanished from the earth tomorrow—and I pray that never happens—Christianity would go on undiminished. We would be sad, but we would lose nothing of our faith.

Antioch was next on our list, because it was the place where the followers of Christ were first called Christians. It was a city where Greek and Jewish cultures met and cross-pollinated. Some of the greatest Christian thinkers of all time came out of Antioch—people who were schooled in both the Jewish and the Greek traditions and knew how to use what was good in Greek culture to spread the truth Christ taught us.

Antioch was famous especially for its style of biblical interpretation. The school of Antioch, as historians call it, emphasized the literal meaning of the texts in Scripture. That was an important contribution to Christian thought at a time when Gnostics and other heretics were running wild with symbolism and mythology. The Christian writers from Antioch teach us to understand the literal meaning of the words *first*, before we go looking for any symbols or allegories.

Yet some thinkers in Antioch may have been *too* literal-minded. Arius, the founder of the Arian heresy, was educated in Antioch. Nestorius was trained in Antioch too. From both of them, we can learn the lesson that too much of even a good thing is *too much*.

Rome, the Eternal City, has been a constant presence throughout our story. It was the center of the empire, and it was where Peter took his seat, making the imperial capital the capital of the Church as well.

All roads led to Rome, and everyone from everywhere came to the capital to do business. Christianity had already arrived there by the time Saint Paul wrote his Letter to the Romans. In fact, as we saw, Christianity arrived before Peter did. But once Peter was there, he made Rome his headquarters, and wherever Peter is, there the Church is.

In the next few centuries, the popes—Peter's successors—solidified their position as leaders of the Christian world by remaining centers of sanity while the storms of controversy raged around them. In the time of the Fathers of the Church, very few great writers and thinkers came out of Rome. Yet over and over, we've seen Christian leaders appealing to Rome when disputes came up. Over and over, we've seen Rome rendering the moderate decision—the *right* decision. Fads in theology washed this way and that over the Christian world, but Rome didn't move. When the latest fad was over, the Church would end up acknowledging that the bishops of Rome had been right all along.

The history we've seen shows us that the Church in Rome had a providential purpose. Catholics believe that the successor of Peter is the head of the Church, the vicar of Christ on earth. But any student of history who looks at the events objectively might come to the same conclusion. When the world went mad, Rome stayed sane. When the Christian Church was in danger of running off the rails, it was always Rome that kept it on track. From our visit to Rome, we learn that we look to Rome as the center.

Alexandria was a place where we saw how easily the Church could run off the rails. In a city that loved a riot, every point of Christian theology could stir up a mob on both sides. Yet Alexandria was also the place most attractive to anyone who really wanted to study Christian theology. No other city had an intellectual tradition like Alexandria's. Thanks to the Ptolemys, it had become a haven for scholars from all over the Greek-speaking world, and that tradition continued into Christian times. People like Clement of Alexandria argued that it was legitimate for Christians to take over whatever was good in pagan Greek culture and use it for the good of the Church.

With so many great Christian thinkers, Alexandria came to have its own tradition in biblical interpretation—one that was almost opposite to Antioch's. The Jewish theologian Philo of Alexandria had shown the way: look beyond the literal meaning of any passage in the Bible to find a symbolic or allegorical meaning. Origen, the most prolific writer in the ancient world, sometimes took this method to extremes.

Yet Alexandria also stood firmly for orthodoxy against Arius, one of Alexandria's own priests. When the Arian heresy burst onto the Christian scene, it was Athanasius—bishop of Alexandria—who formulated the response of the whole Church. No matter how many times he was exiled, Athanasius stood firm. When we talk about orthodox Christianity today as opposed to the Arian kind, we talk about "Athanasian" Christianity.

From Alexandria, then, we get the theological formulas that define our faith, and we also get the second principle of biblical interpretation: Scripture is a deep ocean of meaning.

Ephesus was the place where Saint John the Evangelist lived for many years, teaching his disciples the things Jesus had taught him. Those teachings rippled throughout the Christian world, carried by people who had known John and passed down to the people who knew the people who had known John.

Saint Paul wrote a letter to the Church in Ephesus, and it gives us some of his most beloved passages—especially the one we read at weddings all the time.

Ephesus was also famous for its devotion to the Blessed Virgin. Tradition says she had spent her last days on earth there with the Apostle John. When Nestorius came along and insisted Mary could not *technically* be called "Mother of God", the council that settled the question was held in Ephesus.

From Ephesus, we learn the important principle that you don't mess with the Mother of God.

Edessa opens up the world of Eastern Christianity to us—a world that Westerners are still only beginning to rediscover. The story that its king corresponded with Jesus himself is probably a myth—although we can't always dismiss ancient legends like that, since more than one of them has turned out to be true when a few long-lost ancient documents have turned up. But what it tells us is an important truth—that the Syriac Christianity of the

East looked to Edessa as its birthplace, the city that shaped its traditions.

Edessa also gave us Ephrem, known to Westerners as Saint Ephrem the Syrian, who showed us a different way of dealing with the complexities of theology—a way that used metaphor and poetry to reach out to our hearts as well as our minds. After the long technical arguments with Arius and Nestorius, it's refreshing to turn to Ephrem and enjoy the sheer pleasure of theology as music.

From Edessa, then, we take the lesson that there are different ways of looking at our faith—ways we may not have thought of, but ways that open up a new kind of joy for us when we discover them.

Lugdunum, today's Lyon, is a city most people who aren't specialists don't think of among the great cities of the ancient world. But as the capital of Roman Gaul, it had enormous power and influence. Remember that Roman Gaul is today's France—a country that speaks a language derived from Latin, because Roman power was so thoroughly established there. It was a place where people from all over the empire came to exchange goods and ideas.

Naturally, Christianity was one of those ideas that came into the city from the East, and Lugdunum enters Christian history as the scene of the trials of the martyrs, especially Saint Blandina, the most heroic of them all.

Lugdunum also gave us Saint Irenaeus, whom we call Saint Irenaeus of Lyon. He wrote an encyclopedia of the Christian heresies of his time, explaining what each one taught and why it was wrong. Irenaeus had come from Smyrna, where he knew Polycarp, the disciple of the Apostle John. Thus, he brought a direct apostolic tradition with him when he came to the West.

In writing his book *Against Heresies*, Irenaeus had to make careful distinctions between truth and falsehood. But that didn't prevent him from having fun with his material and sometimes making a joke of the abstruse mythology of the Gnostics. So maybe we can take two lessons from Lugdunum: first, there is a providential purpose even to heresy, which makes us think carefully about what we believe; and second, theology can be fun.

Ejmiatsin, or Vagharshapat, the city with two names, is definitely the one least likely to come up in conversation in the West, if only because we're afraid to make fools of ourselves by trying to pronounce either name. But we can hardly overstate how important it is to scholars of the Church Fathers. The Armenian Church methodically translated all the important Christian books into Armenian so that Armenian Christians could have the best explanations of the faith available. By doing that, they preserved many works of the Fathers that we clumsy Westerners had lost in our stumbling through the centuries. From Ejmiatsin, then, we learn how important it is to hold on to our traditions and how much future generations will thank us if we do.

Constantinople was the imperial capital, the richest city in the world at its height, and the center of all political power. The most talented Christian preachers and thinkers were attracted by its opportunities, and a long list of great figures entered the imperial service and suffered the consequences of imperial proximity. In Constantinople, the drama of state versus church was played out constantly, and in the short term, the state usually came out on top. Yet in spite of all the sufferings of the bishops of Constantinople, the Church won in the end. The Roman Empire in the East is gone; the Church in the East survives.

From Constantinople, then, we learn to be careful what we wish for. Many Christians have wished for the government to be more friendly to their religion. Constantinople shows us what can happen when the government gets too friendly.

Milan was the imperial capital of the West—the place where the emperor had his court and therefore a place that attracted the most talented people. When Ambrose was chosen bishop before he was even baptized, he could easily have sat back and enjoyed a comfortable position with a good salary and a high-class social life. But instead he took his Christian faith seriously and gave all his formidable talents to the Church.

From Milan, then, we learn how powerful it is when Christians make use of their skills and abilities for the faith instead of separating their religious and secular lives. In the case of Ambrose, the combination was powerful enough to make the emperor of Rome kneel as a penitent.

Ravenna was the last refuge of cowardly emperors, the capital of barbarian kings, and the station for the Byzantine provincial government. Peter Chrysologus is probably its most important Christian figure—a man who taught us that the way to make a point to a Christian audience is to keep it short.

For Christian history, however, the most valuable aspect of Ravenna is the art and architecture in the city. Because Ravenna changed less than almost any other ancient city in the West, it keeps several beautiful churches filled with mosaic pictures—not just pictures of Christian scenes but also portraits of the great figures of the day. Other cities have taught us valuable lessons about our faith, but Ravenna shows us what it was actually like to be a Christian at the dawning of the age of Christendom.

And finally, *Carthage*, the capital of Roman Africa, sits at the root of Western Christianity. When Rome was still Greek-speaking as far as the Christian Church was concerned, Carthage was already developing a Latin tradition.

All the earliest Christian writers in Latin came from North Africa. Saint Augustine was a proud African—and he is probably the most famous Western Christian writer of all time and definitely the one most quoted by the *Catechism of the Catholic Church*. Wherever the Latin Rite Mass is celebrated, and wherever theologians use Saint Augustine's terms to explain what the faith means, we are mining the gold from the deep vein of North African Christianity. From Carthage, we take our Western Catholic liturgy and our Western Catholic habits of thought.

Each of these cities contributed to the world of Christian ideas. We might say each one had a providential purpose. We needed both Antioch *and* Alexandria to show us how to read the Bible—understanding the literal meaning first and then finding a message beyond the literal. We needed Constantinople to keep the world safe for Christianity at vital moments but also to show us that when the Church and the state get too cozy, the Church becomes the pawn of the state. We needed Ejmiatsin to preserve some of the writings of the Fathers against all odds when the original Greek versions had long been lost. We needed Carthage to develop a distinctly Western form of Christian liturgy and thought.

One of the most important lessons we've learned from these cities, though, is that places ultimately don't matter. Several of them have vanished; others no longer have a significant Christian presence. Yet the Christian faith goes on. Every one of these cities had an influence on Christian history. But its influence was on how the faith made its way through the world, what interesting traditions it picked up along the way, and how we express the ideas that Christ taught us. Those ideas themselves don't change, and they would be the same if we had removed any one of these cities from the map.

So we have a paradox. Cities matter and they don't matter. The geography of Christian history has shaped the way Christians pray, how we celebrate the Mass, how we think about the eternal truths Jesus told his disciples to teach the whole world. But those truths are the same everywhere, no matter how we express them.

Maybe the most important lesson we can take from all this history, then, is to treasure our own traditions but to be flexible about them. Every individual parish represents a tradition of Christian thought. Yet parishes are not forever. In Africa and parts of Asia, the Church is growing so fast that parishes have to be split in order to keep up. In North America, we've seen drastic parish reorganizations, made necessary by declining numbers and changing lifestyles. We're sad to see our old parishes merge or close, but we carry with us a little of the past into the unknown future.

And that future is not really unknown. Scripture teaches us the ultimate end of the story, and history confirms it for us. We win. The Church goes on until the end of time. Individual members, parishes, and whole cities come and go, but the Church goes on until we are all with Christ in what Scripture describes as the heavenly city—the New Jerusalem.

BIBLIOGRAPHY

Many of these sources are not quoted in the text of this book, but they are useful for background information.

Agathangelos. "History of St. Gregory and the Conversion of Armenia". Milestones (electronic library). Accessed August 8, 2023. http://www.vehi.net/istoriya/armenia/agath angelos/en/AGATHANGELOS.html.

Ambrose. *Letter* 51. Translated by H. de Romestin, E. de Romestin, and H. T. F. Duckworth. In *Nicene and Post-Nicene Fathers*, 2nd series, vol. 10, edited by Philip Schaff and Henry Wace. Buffalo, N.Y.: Christian Literature Publishing, 1896. Revised and edited for New Advent by Kevin Knight. http://www.newadvent.org/fathers/340951.htm.

Aucher, P. Pascal. *A Grammar, Armenian and English*. Venice: Armenian Press of St. Lazarus, 1832.

Augustine, *Confessions*. Translated by J. G. Pilkington. In *Nicene and Post-Nicene Fathers*, 1st series, vol. 1, edited by Philip Schaff. Buffalo, N.Y.: Christian Literature Publishing, 1887. Revised and edited for New Advent by Kevin Knight. http://www.newadvent.org/fathers/110105.htm.

Beacham, Richard C. *Spectacle Entertainments of Early Imperial Rome*. New Haven and London: Yale University Press, 1999.

Boissière, Gustave. *L'Algérie Romaine*. Paris: Hachette et cie, 1883.

Bouchier, E. S. *Life and Letters in Roman Africa*. Oxford: B. H. Blackwell, 1913.

———. *A Short History of Antioch, 300 B.C.–A.D. 1268*. Oxford: Basil Blackwell, 1921.

Brandenburg, Hugo. *Ancient Churches of Rome from the Fourth to the Seventh Century: The Dawn of Christian Architecture in the*

West. Bibliothèque De L'antiquite Tardive series. Turnhout, Belgium: Brepols Publishers, 2005.

Burkitt, F. C. *Early Eastern Christianity.* London: John Murray, 1904.

———. *Euphemia and the Goth: With the Acts of Martyrdom of the Confessors of Edessa.* London and Oxford: Published for the Text and Translation Society by Williams and Norgate, 1913.

Bustacchini, Gianfranco. *Ravenna: Mosaics, Monuments, and Environment.* Ravenna: Cartolibreria Salbaroli, 1984.

Byron, George Gordon. *Lord Byron's Armenian Exercises and Poetry.* Venice: In the island of S. Lazzaro, 1870.

Casson, Lionel. *The Ancient Mariners: Seafarers and Sea Fighters of the Mediterranean in Ancient Times.* 2nd ed. Princeton: Princeton University Press, 1991.

Chandler, Tertius. *Four Thousand Years of Urban Growth: An Historical Census.* Lewiston, N.Y.: St. David's University Press, 1987.Chrysostom, John. *Homily 2 on the Statues.* Translated by W. R. W. Stephens. In *Nicene and Post-Nicene Fathers,* 1st series, vol. 9, edited by Philip Schaff. Buffalo, N.Y.: Christian Literature Publishing, 1889. Revised and edited for New Advent by Kevin Knight. http://www.new advent.org/fathers/190102.htm.

———. *Homily 69 on Matthew.* Translated by George Prevost. Revised by M. B. Riddle. In *Nicene and Post-Nicene Fathers,* 1st series, vol. 10, edited by Philip Schaff. Buffalo, N.Y.: Christian Literature Publishing, 1888. Revised and edited for New Advent by Kevin Knight. https://www .newadvent.org/fathers/200169.htm.

———. "In Kalendas—On the Kalends of January". Translated by Seumas Macdonald. Tertullian.org. Commissioned by Roger Pearse, 2010. https://www.tertullian.org/fathers /chrysostom_in_kalendas.htm.

Chrysologus, Peter. *Letter to Eutyches.* In *Saint Peter Chrysologus: Selected Sermons; and Saint Valerian: Homilies,* translated by George E. Ganss, S.J. New York: Fathers of the Church, 1953.

Cicero, Marcus Tullius. *For L. Flaccus*. In *The Orations of Marcus Tullius Cicero*. Translated by C. D. Yonge. London: Henry G. Bohn, 1852.

Clayton, Peter A., and Martin Price. *The Seven Wonders of the Ancient World*. New York: Barnes & Noble, 1993.

Clement of Alexandria. *The Stromata*. Translated by William Wilson. In *Ante-Nicene Fathers*, vol. 2, edited by Alexander Roberts, James Donaldson, and A. Cleveland Coxe. Buffalo, N.Y.: Christian Literature Publishing, 1885. Revised and edited by Kevin Knight for New Advent. https://www.newadvent.org/fathers/02101.htm.

Clement. *First Letter of Clement*. Translated by John Keith. In *Ante-Nicene Fathers*, vol. 9, edited by Allan Menzies. Buffalo, N.Y.: Christian Literature Publishing, 1896. Revised and edited for New Advent by Kevin Knight. https://www.newadvent.org/fathers/1010.htm.

Cureton, W., trans. and ed. *Ancient Syriac Documents Relative to the Earliest Establishment of Christianity in Edessa and the Neighbouring Countries, from the Year After Our Lord's Ascension to the Beginning of the Fourth Century*. London and Edinburgh: Williams and Norgate, 1864.

———. *Spicilegium Syriacum, Containing Remains of Bardesan, Meliton, Ambrose, and Mara Bar Serapion*. London: Rivingtons, 1855.

Deutsch, Bernard F. *Our Lady of Ephesus*. Milwaukee: Bruce Publishing, 1965.

Donfried, Karl P., and Peter Richardson. *Judaism and Christianity in First-Century Rome*. Grand Rapids, Mich.: Wm. B. Eerdmans Publishing, 1998.

Downey, Glanville. *Ancient Antioch*. Princeton: Princeton University Press, 1963.

———. *A History of Antioch in Syria: From Seleucus to the Arab Conquest*. Mansfield Centre, Conn.: Martino Publishing, 2009.

Drijvers, H. J. W. *Bardaisan of Edessa*. Assen, Netherlands: Van Gorcum, 1966.

Duval, Rubens. *Histoire politique, religieuse et littéraire d'Edesse jusqu'à la première croisade*. Paris: Imprimerie Nationale, 1892.

Ekonomou, Andrew J. *Byzantine Rome and the Greek Popes: Eastern Influences on Rome and the Papacy from Gregory the Great to Zacharias, A.D. 590–752*. Lanham, Md.: Lexington Books, 2007.

Empereur, Jean-Yves. *Alexandria: Jewel of Egypt*. Discoveries Series. New York: Harry N. Abrams, 2002.

Ephrem the Syrian. *The Pearl*, Rhythm the Second. In *Select Works of S. Ephrem the Syrian*. Translated by J. B. Morris. Oxford: John Henry Parker, 1847.

Eusebius. *Church History*. Translated by Arthur Cushman McGiffert. In *Nicene and Post-Nicene Fathers*, 2nd series, vol. 1, edited by Philip Schaff and Henry Wace. Buffalo: Christian Literature Publishing, 1890. Revised and edited for New Advent by Kevin Knight. http://www.new advent.org/fathers/2501.htm.

————. *Life of Constantine*. Translated by Ernest Cushing Richardson. In *Nicene and Post-Nicene Fathers*, 2nd series, vol. 1, edited by Philip Schaff and Henry Wace. Buffalo, N.Y.: Christian Literature Publishing, 1890. Revised and edited for New Advent by Kevin Knight. http://www.new advent.org/fathers/25023.htm.

Evans, Helen C., Constance Alchermes, Ina Baghdiantz McCabe, Anna Ballian, Sheila R. Canby, Kathrin Colburn, Yolande Crowe, et al. *Armenia: Art, Religion, and Trade in the Middle Ages*. New York: Metropolitan Museum of Art, 2018.

Graham, Alexander. *Roman Africa: An Outline of the History of the Roman Occupation of North Africa; Based Chiefly upon Inscriptions and Monumental Remains in That Country*. London: Longmans, Green, 1902.

Grant, Michael. *The Ancient Mediterranean*. New York: Meridian Books, 1988.

Greek Ecclesiastical Historians of the First Six Centuries of the Christian Era. London: Samuel Bagster and Sons, 1843.

Guarducci, Margherita. *The Primacy of the Church of Rome: Documents, Reflections, Proofs*. San Francisco: Ignatius Press, 2003.

Ignatius of Antioch. *Letter to the Magnesians*. Translated by Alexander Roberts and James Donaldson. In *Ante-Nicene*

Fathers, vol. 1, edited by Alexander Roberts, James Donaldson, and A. Cleveland Coxe. Buffalo, N.Y.: Christian Literature Publishing, 1885. Revised and edited for New Advent by Kevin Knight. http://www.newadvent.org /fathers/0105.htm.

————. *Letter to the Romans*. Translated by Alexander Roberts and James Donaldson. In *Ante-Nicene Fathers*, vol. 1, edited by Alexander Roberts, James Donaldson, and A. Cleveland Coxe. Buffalo, N.Y.: Christian Literature Publishing, 1885. Revised and edited for New Advent by Kevin Knight. https://www.newadvent.org/fathers/0107.htm.

————. *Letter to the Trallians*. Translated by Alexander Roberts and James Donaldson. In *Ante-Nicene Fathers*, vol. 1, edited by Alexander Roberts, James Donaldson, and A. Cleveland Coxe. Buffalo, N.Y.: Christian Literature Publishing, 1885. Revised and edited for New Advent by Kevin Knight. https://www.newadvent.org/fathers/0106.htm.

Irenaeus. *Against Heresies*. Translated by Alexander Roberts and William Rambaut. In *Ante-Nicene Fathers*, vol. 1, edited by Alexander Roberts, James Donaldson, and A. Cleveland Coxe. Buffalo, N.Y.: Christian Literature Publishing, 1885. Revised and edited for New Advent by Kevin Knight. http://www.newadvent.org/fathers/0103.htm.

————. *Five Books of S. Irenaeus, Bishop of Lyons, Against Heresies*. Translated by Members of the English Church. Oxford: James Parker, 1872.

Jeremias, Joachim. *Jerusalem in the Time of Jesus: An Investigation into Economic and Social Conditions during the New Testament Period*. Philadelphia: Fortress Press, 1969.

Jerome. *Letter 127*. Translated by W. H. Fremantle, G. Lewis and W. G. Martley. In *Nicene and Post-Nicene Fathers*, 2nd series, vol. 6, edited by Philip Schaff and Henry Wace. Buffalo, N.Y.: Christian Literature Publishing, 1893. Revised and edited for New Advent by Kevin Knight. http://www.newadvent.org/fathers/3001127.htm.

Josephus, Flavius. *Josephus*. Cambridge: Harvard University Press; London: William Heinemann, 1926.

————. *The Works of Flavius Josephus*. London: G. Bell and Sons, 1889.

Justin, *Dialogue with Trypho* 142. Translated by Marcus Dods and George Reith. In *Ante-Nicene Fathers*, vol. 1, edited by Alexander Roberts, James Donaldson, and A. Cleveland Coxe. Buffalo, N.Y.: Christian Literature Publishing, 1885. Revised and edited for New Advent by Kevin Knight. http://www.newadvent.org/fathers/01289.htm.

Kondoleon, Christine. *Antioch: The Lost Ancient City*. Princeton: Princeton University Press, 2000.

Krautheimer, Richard. *Rome: Profile of a City, 312–1308*. Princeton: Princeton University Press, 2000.

————. *Three Christian Capitals: Topography and Politics*. Berkeley, Los Angeles, and London: University of California Press, 1983.

Lactantius, Lucius Caecilius Firmianus. *God's Judgments upon Tyrants: Or a History of the Wicked Lives and Remarkable Deaths of Those Roman Emperors Who Persecuted the Primitive Christians. Written Originally in Latin by Lactantius. Made English by the Right Reverend Father in God Gilbert (Burnet) Lord Bishop of Sarum. By Whom Is Prefix'd, a Full View of Popery, in a Large Preface concerning Persecution*. 2nd ed. London: Printed for J. Roberts near the Oxford Arms in Warwick Lane, 1715.

Leon, Harry J. *The Jews of Ancient Rome*. Philadelphia: Jewish Publication Society of America, 1960.

McClure, M. L. (Herbert), and Charles Lett Feltoe, trans. and eds. *The Pilgrimage of Etheria*. London: Society for Promoting Christian Knowledge; New York: Macmillan, 1919.

Milne, J. G. *A History of Egypt under Roman Rule*. Vol. 5 of *A History of Egypt*. London: Methuen, 1924.

Nicolai, Vincenzo Fiocchi, Fabrizio Bisconti, and Danilo Mazzoleni. *The Christian Catacombs of Rome: History, Decoration, Inscriptions*. Regensburg: Schnell & Steiner, 2002.

Paton, W. R., trans. *The Greek Anthology*. London: William Heinemann, 1916.

Peters, Francis E. *Jerusalem: The Holy City in the Eyes of Chroniclers, Visitors, Pilgrims, and Prophets from the Days of Abraham to the Beginnings of Modern Times.* Princeton: Princeton University Press, 1995.

Phillips, George, ed. and trans. *The Doctrine of Addai, the Apostle.* London: Trübner, 1876.

Philo of Alexandria. *The Works of Philo Judaeus.* Translated by C. D. Yonge. London: Henry G. Bohn, 1855.

Pixner, Bargil. *With Jesus in Jerusalem: His First and Last Days in Judea.* Rosh Pina, Israel: Corazin, 1996.

Portella, Ivana Della. *Subterranean Rome.* Cologne: Könemann, 2000.

Poulin, P. Eugene. *The Holy Virgin's House: The True Story of Its Discovery.* Istanbul: Arıkan Yayınları, 1999.

Pratten, Benjamin Plummer, and William Cureton. *Syriac Documents Attributed to the First Three Centuries.* Edinburgh: T. & T. Clark, 1871.

Procopius. *Procopius.* Translated by H. B. Dewing. Cambridge, Mass.: Harvard University Press, 1914.

Quatman, G. William. *The Tomb of the Virgin: A Compilation of Writings on Mary's Final Earthly Days.* Kansas City, Mo.: Ephesian Press, 2012.

Reid, James S. *The Municipalities of the Roman Empire.* Cambridge: Cambridge University Press, 1913.

Romer, John, and Elizabeth Romer. *The Seven Wonders of the World: A History of the Modern Imagination.* New York: Barnes & Noble, 2005.

Rosovsky, Nitza, ed. *City of the Great King: Jerusalem from David to the Present.* Cambridge, Mass.: Harvard University Press, 1996. See esp. chap. 1, "The Inhabitants of Jerusalem", by Magen Broshi.

Scholasticus, Socrates. *Ecclesiastical History.* Translated by A. C. Zenos. In *Nicene and Post-Nicene Fathers,* 2nd series, vol. 2, edited by Philip Schaff and Henry Wace. Buffalo, N.Y.: Christian Literature Publishing, 1890. Revised and edited for New Advent by Kevin Knight. http://www.new advent.org/fathers/2601.htm.

———. *The Ecclesiastical History of Socrates, Surnamed Scholasticus, Or the Advocate: Comprising a History of the Church in Seven Books, from the Accession of Constantine, A.D. 305, to the 38th*

Year of Theodosius II, Including a Period of 140 Years. London: George Bell and Sons, 1874.

Segal, J. B. *Edessa, "The Blessed City".* Oxford: Clarendon Press, 1970.

Sozomen, and Photius I, Patriarch of Constantinople. *The Ecclesiastical History of Sozomen: Comprising a History of the Church from A.D. 324 to A.D. 440*, trans. Edward Walford. London: Henry G. Bohn, 1855.

Stevenson, James. *The Catacombs: Life and Death in Early Christianity.* Nashville, Camden, and New York: Thomas Nelson, 1985.

Tertullian, Perpetua, and T. Herbert Bindley. *The Epistle of the Gallican Churches, Lugdunum and Vienna: With an Appendix Containing Tertullian's Address to Martyrs and the Passion of St. Perpetua.* London: Society for Promoting Christian Knowledge, 1900.

Testa, Emmanuel. *The Faith of the Mother Church.* Jerusalem: Franciscan Printing Press, 1992.

Thackeray, H. St. J. *The Letter of Aristeas: Translated with an Appendix of Ancient Evidence of the Origin of the Septuagint.* London: Society for Promoting Christian Knowledge, 1917.

Thomson, R. W. "Agathangelos". In *Encyclopædia Iranica.* Vol. 1, fasc. 6, pp. 607–8. Article originally published December 15, 1984; online edition, 2011. http://www.iranica online.org/articles/agathangelos.

Tixeront, J. *Les origines de l'Église d'Édesse et la légende d'Abgar: étude critique; suivie de deux textes orientaux inédits.* Paris: Maisonneuve et Ch. Leclerc, 1888.

Wallace-Hadrill, D. S. *Christian Antioch: A Study of Early Christian Thought in the East.* Cambridge: Cambridge University Press, 2008.

Wilkinson, John. *Jerusalem as Jesus Knew It: Archaeology as Evidence.* London: Thames and Hudson, 1978.

Yiśra'el, Muze'on. *Cradle of Christianity.* Jerusalem: Israel Museum, 2000.

Zosimus, Johannes Leunclavius, and Photius. *The New History.* Translated by Anonymous and John Henry Freese. Pittsburgh: Serif Press, 2022.